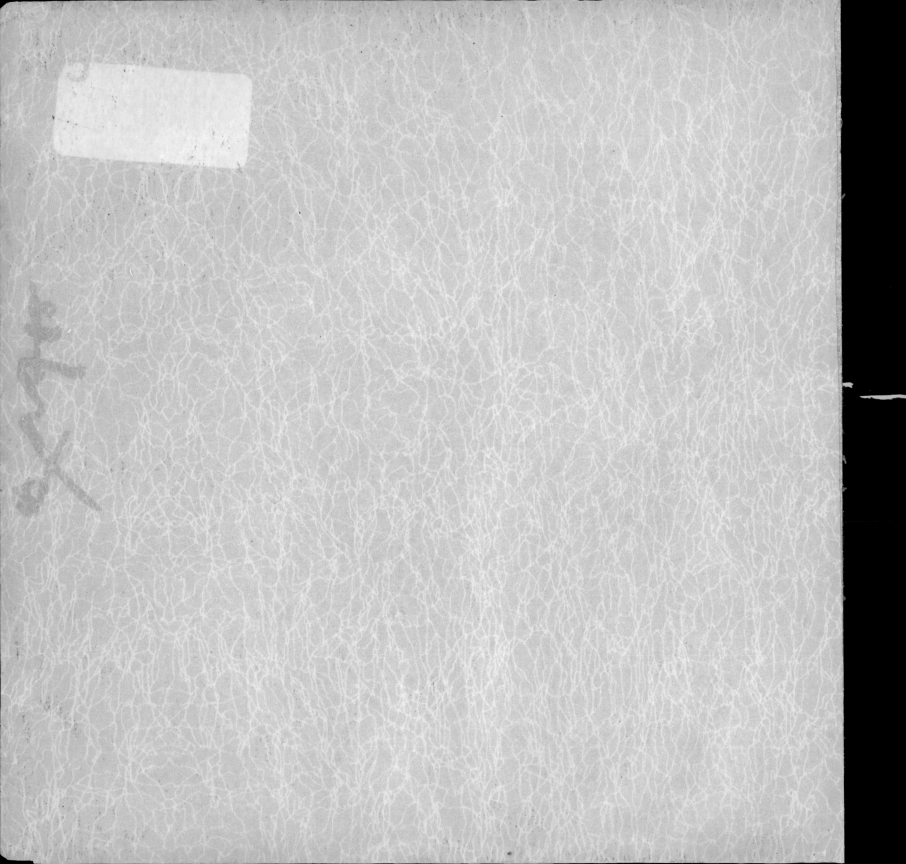

Carmel Art Association
August 4 through September 6, 1994

Catalogue published by the Carmel Art Association

Library of Congress Catalogue Number
94-72075
ISBN 1-88566-07-1

Carmel Art Association
Dolores Street between 5th and 6th
P. O. Box 2271
Carmel, CA 93921
(408) 624–6176

Hours: 10 a.m. to 5 p.m. daily

Typography by Graphically Speaking, Seaside, California
Printed in Hong Kong by AsiaPrint/Everbest

"He was the most complex man I ever knew in my life. I didn't understand him and I don't know anybody that did....In that respect, he was one of the most interesting men I've known."

Steve Crouch,
photographer

FOREWORD

In February, 1993, I began a journey into the past, researching the life of Si–Chen Yuan, a friend, whom I had known during the early 1970s. On this journey, I came across the men and women who had known and loved him. Some wrote their stories, others told them. So with tape recorder, pen and paper, I set forth to wander in and out of the past, accompanied on this voyage by those whom he had touched during his lifetime. It has been a rich, rewarding and often emotional experience. Those people closest to him have relived their parts in his life and the events that led to his death. The impact he had upon those who knew him is as strong today as it was twenty years ago. It has often seemed to me, during these past months, that, were I to turn my head fast enough, I would see him in his old, green sweater and paint–stained jeans, just as charming and dynamic as ever.

He was a man of mercurial temperament, whose emotional swings and sudden impulses controlled his life. A man unable to reconcile his Chinese heritage with the cultural ideas of the Western world. A man to whom pride and honor were of the greatest importance, he was above all, a man totally dedicated to his work, driven to paint and express himself through his art, always striving for greater fulfillment. When he left, it was as though a great life–force, a tremendous energy, had departed, leaving only a terribly empty space.

As both a man and a painter, Yuan enriched our lives with his personality and work. The reminiscences and stories that you read will enable you to travel with me, and know Yuan as did his family and friends. The work you will see in this exhibition and catalogue are part of the legacy he left behind. Participating in this project has truly been a labor of love.

Brenda Morrison
March 1994

24. MONTEREY BAY
   Oil on canvas
   54" x 78"

INTRODUCTION

*S*i–Chen Yuan was born April 4, 1911 in Hangchow, China, in the province of Chekiang. Hangchow, capital of China during the Southern Sung Dynasty, was for centuries a center for the arts. With its legendary West Lake, Hangchow was once thought to be the most beautiful city in China. A morning and evening mist drifts over lake, lush gardens, and mountain views. The Chinese call it, "an earthly paradise." In this lovely and aesthetic environment, Yuan grew up, the eldest of four children born to Pao Ching Yuan, a colonel in the Nationalist Army, and his wife, Sen Pao Sun.

After the birth of his sister, Yu Sun Shen, Yuan was sent to live with his maternal grandparents in Kuchon, 40 miles from Hangchow, where he attended the Wu Ching Elementary School. His sister's birth was followed by that of two more children, brothers, Yu Chi (John) and Yu Jen (Sherman).

An intelligent child, Yuan performed well academically. At an early age, he displayed a keen interest in art, and studied drawing while in high school. This interest was not encouraged by his family, since he was expected to pursue a much more traditional career. Although an artist in China has always had great prestige, the benefactor system for the arts was no longer as strong as it had been before the Republic, therefore it was not easy for an artist to make a good living. Despite the conflict with his parents over his choice of profession, Yuan was eventually permitted to attend the Fine Arts Academy of the Central University in Nanking. There he studied with Xu Beihong, a strong proponent of Western art, and received extensive training in the French academic manner of painting.

Xu Beihong (1896–1953), also known as Peon Ju, was one of China's greatest early twentieth–century painters. Born in I–hsing ,

Yuan's mother, Sen Pao Sun, in China

Kiangsu Province, he studied art at the Shanghai Academy from 1912 to 1918. Shortly after World War I, art schools, influenced by Western ideas, had opened in Peking, Shanghai, Nanking and Hangchow. A visit to Japan in 1917 increased Xu Beihong's interest in Western art, and in 1919 he received a government grant to continue his studies in Paris. Although his grant ran out after four years, he remained in Paris for another six years. In 1928, he returned home to China and became a celebrated pioneer of the modern (Western) art movement. At the time that Yuan attended the Central University at Nanking, Xu Beihong was a professor in the Fine Arts Academy and one of the most influential teachers in China.

Greatly influenced by Xu Beihong, Yuan's art training was almost exclusively in the Western manner. Later, Yuan would remark that though his studies had been in the techniques of the West, he had also been influenced by the Chinese paintings surrounding him and that their delicacy and emphasis upon line were in his blood.

After graduating with a teaching credential, from the art academy at Nanking, Yuan barely had a chance to put his own ideas on canvas before hostilities of the Sino–Japanese War broke out. The Japanese attacked the Chinese forces at Mukden, and seized Manchuria. Together, with most of his generation, Yuan found himself immersed in the years of conflict that were to follow. During that war and World War II, Yuan worked for the Nationalist Government. In 1938, Chiang Kai–shek moved the capital from Nanking to Chungking in Swechuan Province, in southwest China. There, Yuan worked as an artist in the Cultural Department, handling political propaganda. He also was a liaison interpreter for the United States Air Force.

After the war, Yuan returned to eastern China, and by 1947 was living in Shanghai. Long a city of foreign concessions, Shanghai had a very Western and cosmopolitan air. Here, as was often the custom, Yuan adopted an English name. He chose the name Wellington, because he greatly admired the Chinese diplomat, Wellington Koo (Ku Weichun), who was ambassador to the United States, at the time.

One day, a friend, Kai–Zhou Lu, a pilot with the Flying Tigers in the Chinese Air Force, invited Yuan to his family's Shanghai home. There Yuan was introduced to Kai–Zhou's sister, Jen–Chi, whom he would later marry. He became a frequent visitor to the Lu household, and during this time, painted a portrait of Jen–Chi and one of her father, Mu–Tsai Lu. He received the equivalent of $3,000 for this commission. Jen–Chi, who had been studying in the United States, had just graduated from Ohio State. She was home on a visit, before starting her dietician's internship at McGill University in Montreal, Canada. When she again left China in 1948, a correspondence began between her and Yuan.

In 1949, with the Communists taking control of the country, Yuan, too, left China. He accepted an appointment as principal of a Chinese school in Jamaica. In 1950 he applied for, and was granted, a tourist visa to the United States.

After arriving in San Francisco, Yuan held many jobs, including one at the Fairmont Hotel. He was an excellent cook and could express his creativity equally well in the kitchen as on canvas.

Though he was working at a variety of jobs at this time, he still pursued his painting, and in 1951 presented a portrait he had painted of General Douglas MacArthur to the general. It is not known how he came to paint the portrait, nor the circumstances of the presentation.

In 1952 during a visit to the Monterey Peninsula, he was offered a job at the Highlands Inn, in the Carmel Highlands. This was the first time he had seen the Peninsula, and he loved it. He decided that this was where he wished to make his home.

The following year, 1953, was one of great importance for Yuan. He settled on the Monterey Peninsula and obtained a position at the Defense Language Institute teaching Mandarin Chinese. He persuaded Jen–Chi Lu to join him in California, and on May 23rd they were married at the Church of the Wayfarer in Carmel.

Yuan and Jen-Chi on their wedding day

At this time, he was exhibiting his paintings at the Carmel Creamery, a restaurant on the corner of Ocean Avenue and San Carlos Street in Carmel. He also had a showing of his work at the Officers' Mess at the Presidio of Monterey, home of the Defense Language Institute. Of this first exhibition on the Monterey Peninsula, art critic Irene Alexander wrote in the *Herald*, "This exhibition makes a two–edged assault on the observer's interest: first, because it includes a number of works intriguing in themselves, especially in the field of drawing; and second, because it affords an excellent means of tracing the gradual merging of Oriental and Western techniques in art." She went on to say, "Certain Oriental features are traceable in almost everything he paints...in the illumination of a wave, in the details or design of a tree."

In 1954 their daughter, Rae, was born, and Yuan and Jen–Chi purchased a modest home in Pacific Grove. Effort had been made to buy a property in Pebble Beach, but the sale was not completed. Yuan believed this was because they were Chinese and felt there was a great deal of prejudice towards his people.

Daughter Rae posing

Yuan left the Defense Language Institute in 1955, and with the support of his wife, embarked upon a full–time career as a painter. He opened a gallery on Alvarado Street in downtown Monterey, and became a member of the Carmel Art Association. Though most of his paintings were in the Western style, he also painted in the traditional Chinese manner. The early Western style paintings were signed, Wellington Yuan.

Also in 1955, Jen–Chi and their daughter Rae moved briefly to San Francisco, where Jen–Chi worked as a dietician at the Stanford Medical Center. Later in the year, she was able to join the staff of the Community Hospital of the Monterey Peninsula, and return home. She continued to work there as a dietician until 1969.

During the war years in China, three major exhibitions of Yuan's work had been held. Now in the United States, he exhibited widely: Cambridge, Massachusetts; Corpus Christi, Texas; Oklahoma City, Oklahoma and throughout California. Locally, his work could be found, at various times, at Zantman's Gallery, Laky

Gallery, Galerie de Tours and always at the Carmel Art Association. Though he often entered his work in competitives, and won numerous Best–of–Show awards and blue ribbons, he did not keep records of his prizes.

On one occasion he was awarded a blue ribbon at the 1959 Monterey County Fair for a painting he submitted under the name of "Zambini." His paintings had usually been well received at the County Fair and this time he was worried that the new abstract style that he was trying out, would not appeal to the judges. Therefore he submitted the painting under a pseudonym. He won first prize, and it surprised everyone when he stood up to accept the award.

In 1957 the Yuans sold their house in Pacific Grove and moved to Carmel, purchasing a house on Alta Avenue. That same year, Yuan became a member of the Society of Western Artists.

In 1958, after the death of their second child, who had been born with a congenital heart defect, Yuan threw himself into designing and opening a restaurant and new gallery. Located on Cannery Row in Monterey, it was simply called Yuan's. The space was divided between the restaurant, featuring fine Peking cooking, and the gallery with Yuan's paintings stacked against the wall. Unable to paint, grieving for the loss of their child, the restaurant occupied much of his energy. He painted wall panels, designed and built light fixtures. Jen–Chi who worked from 7:00 A.M. to 3:00 P.M. at Community Hospital, would arrive late in the afternoon to help plan and cook the evening's menu. Sadly there was little demand at that time for fine Chinese food and after a time the business closed.

Yuan's first one–man show at the Carmel Art Association was held in 1958 and was very well received. *Herald* art critic, Irene Alexander called it, "A graceful meeting of East and West." For this show, he presented two separate groups of paintings, one in the Chinese manner, and the other his Western–style oils. Alexander wrote in her review, "Yuan is advancing surely and steadily in his painting, to which he now devotes all of his time.

Yuan, Jen-Chi, Rae and friend

Less and less preoccupied with the recording [of] nature in his seascapes and landscapes, he works with growing skill in selection and balance, in pleasing accent, subtlety of texture and boldness of stroke....His hand is always guided by innate taste."

Yuan much admired the works of California artists William Ritschel and Armin Hansen, and England's Frank Brangwyn. Of the Oriental artists, traditional Chinese painters, Kwan Tung, Ma Yuan and Shih Tao were his favorites. In one way or another, all had a considerable influence on his work.

The 1960s was a period of numerous shows, awards and the beginning of his travels to Europe and Mexico. He also opened two different galleries in Carmel, one on San Carlos Street (1965) and the second in Su Vecino Court, on Dolores Street (1968). Yuan never kept his galleries for very long. Either there was a better location, or a new idea to pursue.

Yuan and Jen-Chi in Mexico

Of his travels to Mexico, he said, that he had been especially stimulated and inspired by the Mexican landscape and its people, and felt that Mexico was the land for an artist. The searching and discovering gave him the fulfillment he had dreamed of so long. Europe, particularly Italy, was another favorite. He made three trips to Europe, the last being in 1972.

In 1965, Yuan became a U. S. citizen. His legal status in the United States had been uncertain for many years, and it was not until the McCarren–Walter Act of 1952 was amended by President Johnson in 1965, that Yuan, his wife and other Chinese were able to obtain citizenship.

Having won the Best–in–Show award in 1967 at the Monterey Peninsula Museum of Art, Yuan was given a one–man show at the Museum's Carmel gallery in 1968. Again, Irene Alexander, *Herald* art critic, called the show, "A singularly moving exhibition, containing as it does a series of haunting designs executed in oil and collage and a new, more subtle palette." She felt that, "Yuan [had] truly found his own, individual means of expression, in which the charm and delicacy of his Oriental heritage is melded with a widening horizon gained through recent travel abroad."

In 1969, the Yuans opened the Merry Peach restaurant, at the mouth of Carmel Valley. Jen–Chi left her position at Community Hospital to work with Yuan in their new venture. Yuan cooked and painted at the restaurant and the walls were hung to the ceiling with his paintings. Although he was an accomplished chef, Yuan was uncomfortable being seen working in the kitchen. He felt his stature as a fine artist would suffer. Therefore, he re–designed the interior of the restaurant, so that only a small space, about six inches high, existed through which the chef would pass a customer's order into the dining room. On one occasion, fellow artist, John Morse, jokingly said he was not only an artist but a very good cook. Yuan was very offended, perceiving the comment to be an insult. The business, however, was a necessity, for it provided support for the family and financed Yuan's travels.

Although Yuan was a gifted, prolific and compulsive artist, always searching for new ideas and inspiration, he could be temperamental, moody, and very emotional. Given to acting upon sudden impulse, he had problems dealing with galleries, gallery owners and the general public, regardless of the fact, it was they who supported him by purchasing his work. His erratic pricing of his paintings and drawings, also helped to undermine his ability to make sales.

By 1972, Jen–Chi and Yuan were experiencing problems in their marriage. In an effort to improve the situation, Yuan hired an architect, Walter Burde, to design a new house for them, and they purchased a lot on Mar Monte Street in Carmel. Although their personal problems continued to grow, Yuan continued painting and exhibiting. 1972 was the year of his last one–man show at the Pacific Grove Art Center.

Before construction of the house had begun, Yuan spent much of his time on the property, painting the pine trees that forested the land. A number of the paintings that were in his last exhibition at the Carmel Art Association were those painted there.

Yuan in Italy

In the spring of 1974, the house was completed, but Jen–Chi and Yuan had separated by then. Yuan turned to many of his artist friends for support and encouragement. His work continued to remain of prime importance and he painted with a passion, putting all his energy onto the canvas. These paintings constituted some of the finest work he ever accomplished.

Despondent over what he felt was lack of recognition for his work, his inability to become nationally known, and his failing marriage, he hung his last show at the Carmel art Association on the evening of September 4, 1974. After a visit to his brother, John, he returned home. The next day, he took his own life and died September 6, 1974.

Wellington Si–Chen Yuan's subtle, but colorful palette, vigorous brush strokes, thick impasto and delicate washes are part of the legacy he left. Curiously, despite all his recognition, the Chinese character on his chop translates, "No name." A dynamic, charismatic man and one of California's finest artists, he once said, "Art should have something to say to the viewer, and only then is it honest art, which has permanent value." His art has something to say.

Chronology

1911	Born in Hangchow, China, April 4.
	Graduated from high school. Studied under Xu Beihong at Fine Arts Academy of Central University at Nanking, graduating with a teaching certificate.
The War Years	Worked for the Nationalist Government as a propaganda artist and as an interpreter for the U. S. Air Force in southwest China.
1947	Living in Shanghai. Met future wife, Jen–Chi Lu at her brother's home in Shanghai. Painted her portrait.
1949	Left China for Jamaica, to become principal of a Chinese school.
1950	Arrived in the U. S. on a tourist visa. Worked in San Francisco, including a job at the Fairmont Hotel.
1951	Presented portrait he had painted of General Douglas MacArthur to the general.
1952	Came to the Monterey Peninsula to work at the Highlands Inn in Carmel.
1953	Started teaching Mandarin Chinese at the Defense Language Institute. Married Jen–Chi Lu in Carmel. Had show of his work at the Defense Language Institute.

1954	Purchased house in Pacific Grove.
	Daughter Rae was born.

1955   Left Defense Language Institute to paint full time.
       Opened gallery on Alvarado Street in Monterey.
       Jen–Chi and Rae move briefly to San Francisco.
       Becomes member of the Carmel Art Association.

1957   Sold house in Pacific Grove and purchased house on
       Alta Avenue, Carmel.
       Became member of the Society of Western Artists.

1958   Second child dies as an infant.
       Opened restaurant and gallery, called Yuan's, on
       Cannery Row.
       First one–man show at the Carmel Art Association.

1959   Entered abstract painting in the Monterey County
       Fair under the pseudonym "Zambini", won First
       Prize.

1961   Anna Elizabeth Klumpke Memorial Award, Society
       of Western Artists, M. H. de Young Memorial Mu-
       seum, San Francisco.

1962   One–man show at the Carmel Art Association.

1963   First trip to Europe.

1965   Opened gallery on the east side of San Carlos in
       Carmel.
       Became citizen of the United States.

1966   First Prize, Monterey County Fair.
       City and County of San Francisco Trophy, for Best
       Exhibit in Traditional Art, Monterey County Fair.

1967	Best in Show, Lodi Annual Competitive.
	Best in Show, Monterey Peninsula Museum of Art.
	One-man show, Zantman Galleries, Carmel.
	One–man show at the Carmel Art Association.

1968   One–man Show at the Monterey Peninsula Museum of Art, then in Carmel.
Briefly had a gallery in Su Vecino Court, Dolores Street, Carmel.
Finalist for the National Benedictine Art Award from the American Federation of Arts, Manufacturer's Hanover Trust Gallery in New York.

1969   Opened Merry Peach restaurant, Carmel Rancho Shopping Center.

1972   First Prize, Modern Section for *Pine in Snow* at the Monterey County Fair.
Purchased lot on Mar Monte in Carmel. Architect Walter Burde designed house.
One–man show at the Carmel Art Association.
Last trip to Europe.
One–man show at Pacific Grove Art Center.
One–man show at Laky Gallery, Carmel.

1974   House on Mar Monte in Carmel, completed.
Yuan and his wife separated.
September 4, Yuan hangs last one–man show at the Carmel Art Association.
September 6, dies after committing suicide.

1994   *S. C. Yuan* exhibition, Carmel Art Association.

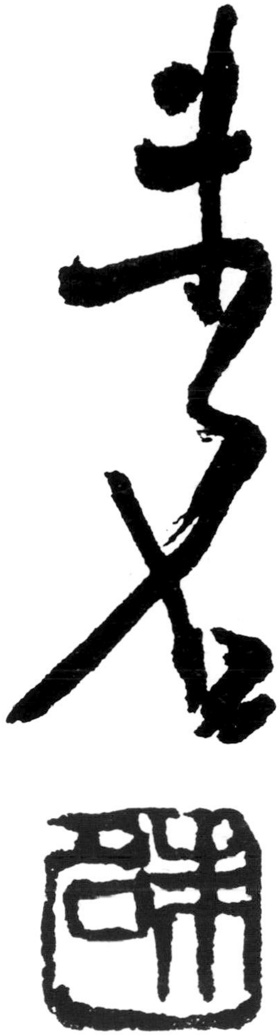

JEN–CHI ANDERSON

Born in China, educated in the United States and Canada, Mrs. Anderson was previously married to S. C. Yuan for twenty–one years. They had one daughter Rae.

From an interview in December, 1993.

We were married at Church of the Wayfarer, in Carmel, May 23, 1953. Two of us, no family there then. Beautiful service, and a friend did the singing.

Yuan sang, he was choosing between artist and conductor. Adored music and I learned to appreciate Mozart from him. Because you know in our restaurant he wouldn't play anything but Mozart. He did some singing when he was teaching, but then he decided he'd better just paint. I think his mother was the one who bought him his first set of paints. Father didn't think it was so good because it is not a good way to make a living. Very practical.

His father, was a colonel in Chiang Kai–shek's Army. Father was severe. In China, a father spanks anytime he feels it's deserved. To someone that's very sensitive it's very harsh. And his father was very important in his mind even though he didn't care for the way his father treated him. His father passed away at sixty–three. And he didn't think he could live longer than his father. Very sad.

Yuan was the eldest child. A daughter born to his parents became the favorite child followed by two sons, John and Sherman. The mother liked the daughter better, so as soon as the mother had the daughter, Yuan was given away to the grandparents. Made him feel very rejected and abandoned. Didn't want him any-

Yuan and Jen-Chi's wedding day,
Wayfarer Church, Carmel

107. UNTITLED
Ink on paper
10 1/2" x 18 1/2"

more. I think he felt that way all through his life. That he was not good enough for the parents to take care of him. It was the saddest part of his whole life. He just felt the Mother loved the daughter very much, and the boys after that were very much well accepted, except he, the oldest son. The only one given to the grandparents. Brothers and sister were close. Yuan was alienated from his brothers and sisters the rest of his life. They took his place in the family.

He felt he's not good enough. So he developed this terrible temper. Everytime he has a temper tantrum then everyone gives in. This was all through all his young life.

Would throw a tea cup from one end of the room to another, nothing new, I would get out of the house because I don't want to have him get worse, but usually by the time I get home he would have cleared it all up. Got over it quickly but then would feel bad to think he did that.

Yuan was a good student. Kindergarten, elementary school, high school for six years. Twelve years education plus four years college. He wrote Chinese very well. You know in China if you can write the characters well you have a very good chance of being recognized and he wrote extremely well. Beautiful, elegant writing.

Started school as a little boy but when the grandparents came to pick him up he felt so bad because other parents were so young and his were old. And he always remembered that. It was very hurtful. Bright child. Extremely intelligent, very fond of music, very fond of painting. Which was not good in Chinese society, unless you have a way to make a living or a benefactor to sponsor you.

Toward the end of life, Yuan stayed with Lim for awhile. He was so hoping someone would take him in permanently. He felt abandoned. So sad. He didn't think he could support himself on the painting sales. Of course, I felt bad, being born and raised in China. I always felt the wife's responsibility to take care of hus-

63. WATERLILIES
Oil on canvas
17" x 48"
Exhibited in Yuan's
last show at Carmel Art
Association, September, 1974

89. GLADIOLAS
Oil on canvas
40" x 40"

Sketching on site

5. ST. MICHAEL'S, PARIS
    Oil on canvas
    30" x 30"

band, no matter what he did. So through the married life I worked and I thought I was being a good wife. I wasn't aware I was taking responsibility away from him and because of that, very seldom do I allow my daughter, Rae to depend on me. That is my greatest regret because I took that, I took that privilege away from him. I always paid the bills, the taxes, paid whatever bills, reasonable or unreasonable, so that he can be spared to paint. But I was not aware that he was unable to make a living on his own. He didn't feel he had the capability. When he went to make a loan, he used my name, because I had a steady job. He couldn't borrow money without using my name, which caused a lot of uncomfortable things at home. He didn't ask me, just went and signed my name, but again being Chinese, I don't want to humiliate my own husband. Go to the bank and say don't loan him any money. But usually it was when he was in Europe then I get the payment loans.

He bought a Porsche. Can you imagine? We lived together and I never knew there was a Porsche! I didn't even know. He kept it in the garage and it was all covered in newspaper. And today, I haven't seen another Porsche of that color. It was sold to an architect. It was a beautiful red. It was a customer who came and said, "What car are you driving now?" I said, "Still the same one." "What color?" "That beige one I've had for years." "Oh no, that's not the car you have." I said,. "What are you telling me?" Right away, I know something is wrong. "Oh," he said, "I shouldn't tell you." Then right away I go home and said to Rae, first I open all the drawers trying to find a key, and so Rae says, "Mom, what are you looking for." I say, "Did you see a new car?" She says, "Yes!" "Where?" "In the garage. It's a brand new Porsche." Brand new special order. And there, two Mercedes and one Porsche! How are we going to pay for it? Can you imagine. A Porsche sports car for Rae, and a sedan for me and there we are paying for restaurants, his trip to Europe, paying for the home, because we mortgaged the home to pay for the restaurant. So I looked at him and said, "How are we going to pay for all this?" He said, "Oh, I just paint a painting and when its sold we pay for everything." He can always think that he will really sell. And he felt so bad because all his friends were selling so well. Even when he sold well he was still depressed. Like he would win a prize, blue ribbon, for five minutes he was delighted, after that he was down again. I said, "How come, aren't you happy, to sell, to celebrate, you just won the first prize." He said, "No, my painting is not good enough". Right away he felt that a certain part of the painting still is not what it should be, and right away he goes to paint again. Painted often, often 'til one or two o'clock in the morning. He could do it better late. And there were times he would paint a painting and say, "You know, I don't know how I did it." He himself couldn't figure how the colors and composition came together. This why when I asked him, "What's this?", he became very disgusted, because this was his feelings. He would say, "This is how I communicate. Don't you understand?" It must have been frustrating for him. But then of course on his own he always felt an artist should be poor. An artist should live in a very poor environment. So often times he would, whether we rent a house or we bought a rather debilitated home, he always get the garage, sort of half fixed up and he always told me, he always told me if he lived in a garage, he could paint much better.

I told him when we were first married the only thing I wanted, I don't want fur coats or diamond rings, I just want to have a home, a house. So toward the very end when he knew that the marriage wasn't doing well, this architect, liked his painting, Mr. Walter Burde, and he asked him to make a design. So while we still having the restaurant, Merry Peach, he was so pleased. They made a model. He brought it to the restaurant. I was so pleased and so happy. I'll be so happy if we can have a home like this. And Keith [Lindberg] used to come here. Before anything was done. They would be here painting pine trees.

After we bought the land, the lady said we'd got to pay it off. The loan was only five years. Then we have to go and borrow money from life insurance. Borrow to buy house. And he was sure if the house was built we'd get back. That was his goal. I wanted so much to have a good marriage, to have a good home. It was my goal. Every step of working toward that he sabotaged that and then we are totally in debt. And the way he buys paint, a whole case of white! It's hard when you don't have food on the table.

55. ABSTRACT
Oil on canvas
32 1/2" x 32 1/2"

87. PORTRAIT OF RAE
Oil on canvas
36" x 35 1/2"

He was a sad person, but I don't think he gave that image to his friends that he was sad, because he could be totally energetic, totally enthusiastic. I remember in the morning, I go to work really early about 7:30 to get to work on time. He would be sitting there, just sitting there really depressed and by the time I come home in the same chair he would still be sitting there, still depressed, though of course, I don't know what he did in between, but I think he wanted me to see that he's very unhappy. Of course at that time without any understanding of myself or anyone else, I took it as my fault. I should be very guilty and do better. But then as I find that the more I did the worse it got; it didn't get any better. Even now I still don't understand. Why if someone is good to you and trying to provide you with an environment so that you can paint and yet you resent it. He really resented it. More and more I felt, I'm not a good wife. I'm not good enough and that didn't help any. Keith [Lindberg] told us to go to a counselor. Keith really did try to help.

The counselor was kind and very nice. He said, "There's no emotion between the two of you. You don't get angry. You don't say anything to him. You just sit there and listen." I said, "You'd really like to see me get angry?", and he said, "Yes. I'd like to see you get angry, to say something to him." I said, "First of all I'm afraid because I don't want to get beaten up." Then I said, "If I said something I may be *so* angry I may say a lot of things that I would regret." Because there was so much bottled up emotionally you know. Finally, we went to see a psychiatrist too. In the later part, the psychiatrist told him he really wanted to see the family together. Evidently this is a dysfunctional family. I thought the counselor was excellent. He taught us the technique of how to communicate and what when something was irritating to do instead of screaming and yelling. Pat his shoulder or he can do something to let me know how he's irritated. But somehow I remember Yuan said, "I just don't know how to love you, I don't know how to say loving things." It frightens him. He says, "I don't know how to call you, 'Dear.' Other people say darling, I don't know how to say that, it can't come out of me." He's so afraid of emotion. And yet his emotion is so explosive.

I always knew his painting would get better.

When our second child was ill and at the end of her life, it affected Yuan *very* bad. When the second child died, he said he couldn't paint anymore. For six months, he built a restaurant for us. Later it was the York restaurant, on Cannery Row, now it's something else. All by himself, o.k., he created a restaurant. No proper kitchen utensils, just a stove, a regular stove, that was already there, and he expected to have a restaurant? But he was happy. He's artistic and he used all his artistic talents in building a very lovely handmade center light, totally made by hand, painted, the whole place was created by him and all the panelings are his paintings and one side is his gallery and the other side is my restaurant. He wanted Rae and me and him together. I would be cooking and serving dinner, making money, and he would be painting on the other side. Cannery Row before it developed and was called Peking Gourmet Dining. And we served authentic Chinese food, which is very different than chop suey or chow mein or egg foo yong. The real delicate Chinese food. He really meant well. He spent all his energy to create that restaurant because the little child died. Because the impact was so strong he couldn't paint. The only painting he painted was of the monastery, a little one. I think at that time, he felt perhaps to go to the monastery would comfort him. You see when the baby died I couldn't cry. He was the one that cried and cried and cried. When we went to the funeral place, he's the one that cried. By then I couldn't cry.

At any rate he really didn't want the child. The interesting part is when the child was born and he went to see the child. Steve Crouch was with him. Took this wonderful portrait of him. The two of them were there and I remember getting my suitcase and driving myself to the hospital to have the baby. Anyway he and Steve were having a wonderful time at home so I just took myself to the hospital. I thought it was just as well, he was so nervous and I didn't know what he would do in the hospital. This way I know everyone there. I didn't see Yuan until, I guess a nurse informed him that he had another girl. And when he came, he told me, "You know it's real strange, I pick up the baby and she

81. TILLIE GORTS
Pen and chalk on paper
9" x 11 1/2"

refuse to look at me, she just turn her head totally to the other side."

At that time, we thought the baby was all right, nobody had told us anything was wrong. And after that I think the baby was fine. But after thirty–six hours the doctor came to tell us that the baby may not live. And Yuan never wanted her anyway. At any rate this baby cost us traveling all over California to save her. And we still couldn't save her. And Yuan had to paint Rae's portrait right then and he was painting with the baby in the crib because she was dying. I had contracted German measles. As a dietician I visited patients in their rooms. I didn't know I was pregnant. So when she born, she was sick. Yuan couldn't handle it. Couldn't paint. Every day he'd call the hospital. The child died and he devoted his whole time to building the restaurant. He wanted his whole family to be together from morning to night.

The restaurant didn't prosper. Days went by without one single customer, because at that time people don't know what real Chinese food is, now they do. But we were the first restaurant that ever served real Chinese food, the real delicate, authentic Chinese food. So then this Chinese man that owned Monte Mart Market came and gave him $6000 from the blue. I was so happy. He said, "Here it is. Here's the money. I'm taking off, going to Europe." That was his first trip. He was commissioned to paint all fruit and vegetable mural for new supermarket, fish. Yuan's paintings on the wall. Monte Mart in Salinas. Painting may still be there.

With this $6000 he went to Europe for the first time. He was going to stay a long time because he had bought all the supplies he possibly could. He put them in a locker. When he went back it was all gone. He had deposited the money and supplies in one of those little lockers. It was all stolen. Italy. The paint and brushes, boxes, etc., were all there, but the money was gone. The first time he went there he was so excited. He ordered an automobile, Mercedes, he wants Mercedes so badly. He wants to present himself, so he buys Italian, tailor–made suits, spent money on me, got the most beautiful leather Italian–made briefcase, ladies, expensive, bought suits for me. I was excited when I

Aboard ship

90. STILL LIFE WITH RED ROSES
Oil on canvas
20" x 16"

received them, but none of them are my size! A size 40! Can you imagine me wearing a size 40? [European size 40] And I had to take them to a tailor to have them fixed, and I have to pay import tax! Expensive suits, at that time. $200 suits are very expensive from Paris. I was excited too, but at the same time, I just felt, don't do it anymore to me. Then he ran out of money, with all the shopping and then he sent a Western Union. He needs money, we had no money. And my daughter said, "I have some money, I'll send it to him." $15.00! And so Mr. Hennessey, an artist, elderly gentleman, sent him some money and of course he had to sell the Mercedes. But of course once you've bought it, and then sell it right away, it's not worth much.

The Mercedes gone, plus he owes money to the Hennesseys when he came back. But to him, his paintings will sell. The European paintings will sell like hot cakes, and he'd be able to be rich and famous and live happily ever after! But unfortunately it didn't happen. It was too bad.

I think at night when Keith [Lindberg] has a class and he could go and attend [Sunset Center Life drawing class, Tuesday evening] then he could go to draw. I think that made him feel good. Then he comes home. By then I'd be already in bed, but I do hear him tear the pages off the drawing book, and they are finished. Then he put them on a hot press so they come under and I would count, one, two. I'd be in another room and would just hear him tearing from the sketch book. There are times, when I would count thirty or more in one evening. Sometimes he doesn't get home until eleven or twelve o'clock. I would get worried, but he often went for coffee with the other artists.

But you know people didn't even know Yuan was married and they didn't know he was married and had a daughter. And Rae was hurt. The Monterey Peninsula Museum of Art, in Carmel at that time, gave him a show. Yuan was being invited by lady artists for lunch in their home and of course he would reciprocate too at lunchtime. I was at work, so who admired him, I don't know, or who he invited. I know Cookie [Crouch] is good friend of his, but in a nice way, artists together, talk about painting.

Aboard the S/S Romantica

30. MERRY PEACH
Oil on canvas
18" x 24"

Cookie knew that he was married and had a daughter, but many of the lady friends, that invite him were really surprised. Yuan wasn't too bad looking, he was sloppy, he can be charming, so charming. Rae heard that some of the ladies didn't know he was married. "But I'm his daughter, I just feel terrible. I feel hurt." That was the first time he took us to any of the awards or shows. By then he was already aware that the marriage was getting bad.

I think his artist friends were much more honest with him than the Chinese family. Later, he did ask his brother, "How come none of you ever told me I wasn't good to my wife." Nobody ever told him you should be good to your wife and daughter. Nobody ever told him. Only the American artists told him. There was one artist named Bishop. Yuan would go to see him and say, "How come she doesn't want me to paint. That's my profession, that's the only thing I know how to do." And the friend said, "Where do you do your painting?" He said, "Sometimes on the kitchen table, sometimes on the dining table, sometimes outside. Every place is my painting." He said, "If you live like that then you shouldn't have a wife." But Yuan said, "Why can't I have a wife and just do what I please?"

I loved the man for his talent, even though sometimes I'm really angry but when I see, every night he brings a painting home, leave it there and say tell me what you think of it. I was scared to death to say anything, because whatever I said is not right. But at any rate, he trained me to appreciate paintings. So now if you give me a painting, I don't know the theory, but I can tell whether that painting is well composed. I can tell if the artist is really together, from that training of twenty–one years.

He graduated from the Nanking University. Graduated art. Teacher Peon Tu or Xu Beihong, one and same. Best teacher. Then he worked. He was commissioned to paint Chiang Kai–shek's portrait and he was rewarded for that, which encouraged him to continue. But of course the war was on . He was almost killed. One day he found himself floating in the river in the central part of China. He didn't know he was alive, but he was. Somebody saved him. But during the war he had a very terrible time.

6. STREET RONDA, OLD RING
Oil on canvas
24" x 30"

I think he was in the service. I don't know his rank. I never saw him in uniform. He was an officer in Chinese Nationalist Army. So were the two brothers. One in the air force, one was a colonel in the Army. Just before the Second World War. Of course during the Second World War, they were still in the service.

After the war he was appointed to be the principal of a Chinese school in Jamaica. It is customary for Chinese people, when they are here [not in China], to go to regular public school in the daytime, and Chinese school at night. So you learn the language. Yuan really was a very talented man. He spoke Mandarin Standard Chinese, he spoke his native dialect, which is of the Chekiang Province, which is where all the Chinese scholars come from, that particular province. Talent in literature, then he speaks Cantonese which is what all the Chinese who immigrated to the U.S. speak. So he got around in China Town, where I can't. A very intelligent man. He come home, if he goes on Chinese New Year's time, and always brings a wrapped red envelope with money, because the Chinese people with his same last name would give him a red envelope to bring back to Rae. But Rae never got it. Rae just dearly loved him, but even now she says, "I don't think I could ever do anything to please my Dad." She's still trying. Rae is like him, emotional and full of energy.

Yuan was very negative in many ways, his belief structure and his attitude. He probably didn't portray that to the people he painted with. He probably portrayed a very successful, macho type of guy. I think he was really a very scared man. He was so frightened, and later toward the very, very end I told him, "I wish I wasn't so scared of you." I said, "How can a wife be frightened of the husband and still can make love with the husband." I was scared to death, if I sat there and heard those footsteps, he walked quite heavily, my heart would jump. I was that frightened. I had to pray to God, not that I'm a super person, I'm not, but I had to pray to God, "Someone help me, because I'm so scared of my husband."

But later he told me, "You're afraid of me, but I'm afraid of you." But the fear is different. I was afraid of his masculine power. So sad. Man and woman don't communicate. ☞

42 UNTITLED
Watercolor on paper
29 1/4" x 15"
Eleanor Hatlo Lusignan commissioned this painting in the 1950s, to hang over a Chinese chest in her home.

71. BREEZE
   Oil on canvas
   39" x 49"

108. THE SEA
Oil on canvas
22" x 31 1/4"

97. GRAPEFRUIT AND GRAPES
    Oil on board
    8" x 10"

9. MARIGOLDS
   Oil pastel on paper
   20" x 16"

DICK CRISPO

Carmel Art Association member, painter, teacher and activist, Dick Crispo met S. C. Yuan in the early 1960s.

From a story written in February, 1994.

I first met S. C. when I was in high school, in about 1961. He had a Mandarin Chinese restaurant on Cannery Row. He did the cooking, the meals went on for hours. Sometimes there would be a half hour between courses. He was a great cook. In 1969, one time at artist Pat Carey's house, he cooked a meal that took four hours to prepare. We all sat down to eat, but Yuan, he left.

I first saw him painting when in high school. I worked for Fred Klepich at Studio Art Supply in Carmel. He came in with a big easel and large canvases and set up in the restaurant area of the Carmel Craft Studios. There he had Cookie Crouch pose for him. The portrait was in oil; went very rapidly. The colors got grayer and grayer, and Cookie didn't seem to move, even though I don't remember her taking a break, or him asking her to. I was amazed at the skill. After, I asked him, "Why so much gray?", he said, "What gray? It's all colors." He was right.

In 1966, Yuan asked me if I wanted to go to San Francisco with him. "Sure," I said, thinking we'd go to art shows; might even eat at a Chinese restaurant that only he knew about. Instead, we drove up to the San Francisco Art Institute's Annual Painting Competition, dropped a painting off, got back in the car and he drove home, in his Chrysler station wagon at a blurr. Foolish me, I thought I was going to San Francisco, for the day, with S. C. Yuan! ✑

73. UNTITLED
    Collage on board
    31" x 26"

48. PIER IN MONTEREY
    Oil on board
    14" x 18"

60. WHARF, MONTEREY
    Oil on canvas
    30" x 59"

36. TREES IN WINTER
     Oil on masonite
     23 1/2" x 23"

Painting in his studio on Alta Avenue

76. CAFÉ RAOUL
Oil on board
18" x 24"

SJEF WILDSCHUT

Born in Holland, Sjef Wildschut became a friend of S. C. Yuan in the early 1960s. He is now a photographer living in Portland, Oregon.

From an interview in April, 1994.

I first met Yuan in 1964, when I was doing my bit with Steve Crouch. I was nineteen, maybe twenty. I was a working student, not allowed to get paid. It was my *stage* year, my practical year. Yuan was a friend of Steve's. They were fantastic friends, good friends.

Yuan and I, we'd have lots of talks. He was a great conversationalist. We'd talk a lot about politics, because here we were, both foreigners. I was a West European and he was from China. We were just having a meeting of the minds, about where the world was going. Our viewpoints were similar. Especially because there was Vietnam at that time. We would exchange thoughts about what was happening over there, that it was very much a civil war, rather than a war against communism. He had wonderful, funny remarks about the atom bomb, "Big toy, big toy, everybody wants one." It was wonderful to discuss politics with him. He never treated me as a younger man. He didn't set himself up as an older man, father–like, a know–it–all person. We were just very interested in each other's thoughts.

He had a wonderful little studio near the Crouch's [Alta Avenue]. And it was filled with work. He was really quite prolific, and really good. To be turning out that kind of painting in that day and age, was quite amazing.

51

Yuan had always liked a couple of photographs that I had taken of an Indian in Taos, New Mexico. We exchanged work. For me, it was a gift, what he did. For those prints, I got a portrait he painted of my former wife, Nancy.

He had wonderful stories. He had travelled to Europe before we met; to Italy. He did it by ocean liner, and he took his Cadillac! It is the funniest story, and I will try to imitate, how he would go click, click, click, "I drive Cadillac. Drive in country, very primitive. When I turn corner, everybody have to take table and chair off street." Because he would not drive the highways, of course, he wanted to see the little streets, the plazas. He had a great nose for that, but his car couldn't get there. He sent his car back.

He was one of the best persons, to whom an artist could show his work, because he would be so honest, but refined and true. Ja. He was very supportive. I would show photographs to him, a lot, and I never felt badly, not even sometimes. I was just beginning to get there. The pieces wouldn't be very good. He would make it feel like something good was going to come out of this. That's the difference. He would say it in such a way, and with such kind eyes, and with such body language, that you would say, "Oh for crying out loud, that's right!" He would take a wonderful photograph, and would look at it, and say, "Oh my this is really beautiful. Two photographs in one shot!" He was very, very kind. I only can say, the way I looked at him, was as a very good, warm person with a blanket always somewhere around to throw over you, with a smile and a grin and a sense of humor. And not the sense of humor of saying something, and then going ho,ho,ho. No not at all. A sense of humor of saying something with a twinkle, and then the lips would crack slightly. And then he would stand up and go do something else. He was really, really neat.

Then when Nancy and I came back from Europe, the whole situation had changed. We came back about three months before he committed suicide. Yuan was going through this fantastically bad time. He was so perplexed by his sense of pride being hurt, by things not going well. He felt dishonored. He felt like he could never go back to China now.

Yuan in Italy

99. CASTROVILLE
Oil on board
9" x 12"

He was building that new house at the time, and it was almost finished. I helped him move his studio. It looked like he had recently been to Mexico, and boy, he had some gorgeous paintings there. He had been really busy with light, with outdoor light, how it would fall on buildings. Aw, but could he paint. And he said, seriously, "See all those paintings we just moved?" There'd be a roomful of them, stacked up. He said, "Give me $10,000, you can have them." I knew I was not going to do it. I didn't have that kind of money to spend. He was doing what you call in Dutch, "building off." It doesn't translate. It is a very careful demolition, like when you break a house down, stone by stone. You know exactly what you are doing, you are trying to give things away, because you know this is going to be the end.

Well, for a while there, I had a problem with it, that he chose to pass on this way. Because he had been talking about it so much to me, and I had said, "Come on, that rushes things a bit." You really can't do something about it. You really can't. When I left Carmel, to go back to Portland, he had said to me, "O.K., Sjef, we probably won't see each other anymore. Good bye. Take care." I got to Portland, and a week later, I heard he had shot himself. It was not a shock that he had done it, because I knew he was prepared for it, but I hoped so much that he had not been in anguish. He was in so much anguish the last few weeks. And that got to me. You see, you always want to be there, especially for really dear people, for friends, for people you really care about. You want to be there just at that moment, so much. You want to be there with that warm blanket, and tell them that it's going to be O.K. That's all you can do for good friends. You cannot live their life, you cannot chew their food, but you can be there, be the warm blanket, and say, "Here, it's going to be O.K." So.

Suicide is rotten, because the people who are left behind all have a feeling that maybe they could have done something different. That then the person would not have killed himself. However, that's very self–centered of us to feel that way, because whatever he did, he had the right, it was his life. And who said it was wrong to do so. Yuan had his own values, because of his own heritage.

He was a very pure person, and held on to his old Chinese values. He wouldn't have been walking around in a Chinese robe or anything like that, but his whole thought process, his thoughts about life, his thoughts about painting, were all based totally on the culture of China, and happily so. If he would have immersed himself into American culture, he would have been painting kids with big eyes! He couldn't do that. He was glad to be in America. He never said, "I want to go back to China, this is bad country." No, no. But he would definitely say sometimes, "America, grow up!"

I have good memories of him and I thank him deeply. He was quite a force for me and a very positive person to have known. If I could, I would have bought all of his paintings, and divvied them out to people I liked, so they would be in safe houses. I have the one of Nancy and an unsigned one. I never would have asked him to sign it. It is a watercolor he did of a person crocheting; one of those little old people sitting outside in Bruges. We were talking of those nice little figures, and he said, "Oh, like that." Sincerely, if you count the strokes, there are only three or four strokes. Bah! He said, "Here, for you." It's a beauty, it's quite large and it reminds me of that Chinese story of the emperor and the cock. The emperor said to a painter, "I really wish you would paint me a beautiful cock." The painter went away and didn't come back for nearly fifty years. And when he came back, he sat in front of the emperor, and with an empty canvas, he went swoosh, swoosh, swoosh, and there was that cock. And the emperor said to the painter, "Why did you wait so long to come and paint me the cock?" "Because it takes a life time." That's what Yuan did with that drawing.

I sincerely wonder, how Yuan would have grown old and especially what he would have been painting. Because the guy never stopped growing. Every month he would come up with something different. He never fell into a rut, at least not that I know of, and it is so difficult not to. He had beautiful, gorgeous discipline, and a young spirit. He was fantastic. I wish that he would have stayed around. ✎

Sjef Wildschut

Contemplating in his studio

16. SYMPHONY OF SUNSHINE
Oil on burlap, mounted on board
30" x 40"

52. BOUGAINVILLEA
   Oil on canvas
   23 1/2" x 71 3/4"

85. RAIN
    Waterolor on paper
    15" x 14"

HITOSHI KONO

Japanese–American, met S. C. Yuan in the late 1950s. He is a general contractor and a student of ceramics.

From an interview in February, 1994.

Both, my wife, Jean, and I met S. C. probably around 1964 or 1965. They used to have a restaurant on Cannery Row; it was a tiny restaurant. They had Peking–style Chinese cooking. Jen cooked, and he helped out. He had a little art displayed there. I don't remember the restaurant, the layout that well, but most of the paintings were on the floor and against the wall.

Jean and I got to know them a little bit better when they opened the Merry Peach restaurant, at the mouth of Carmel Valley. We used to go there every two weeks or so, and go back to the kitchen and talk to both of them. That's when he used to take those jaunts to Europe. That's where, after he came back from one trip, that he did the *Rain in Spain* painting and *The Greek Dancers*.

Most of the time S. C. was very friendly to us. At certain times he was very moody and wouldn't even speak to you. But that's an experience that many who were his acquaintances remember about him. I think his paintings display that moodiness. I always thought that S. C. was always worrying.

As far as the painting goes, I consider him a genius. I always thought that. I put him in the category of being in line with the paintings that the Impressionists did, Van Gogh, Monet. He had that certain instinct to display his thoughts on canvas. He was such an introvert. I'm not quite sure that he socialized that much in the outside world as far as our community goes.

I knew he wanted to be famous. "Kono" he said, "You have to take my paintings to Japan, we have to do something with them." We never did because I was working at my job and didn't have the time. If it had been now, I might have done it.

I had a couple of Chinese vases, and they were twins. He saw them because I brought them over, because he was of Chinese heritage. Shortly after, it must have been about a month before his passing, I took one of the vases and I said, "This is yours". He was really appreciative and said, "Gee, I have to give or return something." Then he passed on. And then Jen Yuan called me and said, "Your vase is here and I want to return it to you." I still have both vases. But he admired them quite a bit. And I thought if he liked them so well, he should have one.

I consider him old generation; he held on to a lot of old ties and superstitions. His father died at the same age [63], and maybe that preyed on his mind. I don't think it takes too much to push a person over the edge sometimes. He was impulsive. Sometimes he'd say, "this painting didn't take me very long". His impulse hit it just right, other times he would struggle with a painting.

He used to lock himself into an area or room, while he was painting, would not speak to anyone for a week. I think his food intake was also very limited at that time. He really shut himself from the world.

I think he just wanted to be famous for his painting. I think money and financial endeavors with S. C. were a means to an end. It really didn't matter that much to him, being super wealthy. He needed the money to paint, to go on trips and do his paintings, because money and S. C. didn't hang around too much. He was not a saver.

The last show he had at the Art Association was quite a departure from what he had done in the past. It was fantastic. The lichen on the trees and the bougainvillea. It was quite a shock to learn about his passing, after he had that show. ✐

103. PORTRAIT
Oil on board
12" x 12"

21. FIGURE ON CHAIR
   Charcoal on paper
   15" x 21"

94. HEAD #1
    Pastel on paper
    15" x 12"

Yuan sketching

19. CHEVRON STATION, CARMEL
   Oil on board
   12" x 16"

DOLORES JOHNSON

Mrs. Johnson and her former husband, Ray, owned Peninsula Power Tool and Supply in the early 1960s and met S. C. Yuan at that time.

From an interview in February, 1994.

I met S. C. Yuan in 1960. Yuan came into the shop to price electric saws so he could learn if it would be feasible for him to make his own frames for his paintings. The business was known as Peninsula Power Tool and Supply, located then on Del Monte in Monterey. We handled wood-working equipment.

He was very, very interesting—wonderful sense of humor—and in talking to him it was decided that perhaps we could trade equipment for paintings, as at that time we got the impression he could not afford to purchase a saw.

Not being familiar with his art at that time, as we had only been on the Peninsula a few months, he graciously invited us to his home on Alta Avenue in Carmel to see his paintings, and at that time we met his lovely wife, Jen and his delightful daughter, Rae. Needless to say we were very impressed with the quality of his work so it was decided to exchange an electric saw that he wanted for one of his paintings.

In the ensuing years we became good friends; consumed interesting and delicious meals at his restaurant-gallery on Cannery Row, as he was an excellent chef.

That same year we also bartered another piece of equipment in exchange for his painting, a portrait of me.

This was a very interesting experience, believe I had three sessions with him. He practically had the painting completed in the first session, but had me come back for "refinements". He used box after box of tissues, and consumed great quantities of cola. Yuan talked continuously about anything and everything, very humorously trying to make me laugh during each session and encouraged me to talk. I believe he did this so that I would relax. After we had the portrait in our home, he stopped by one day unexpectedly, came in, looked at the portrait said, "yes" picked up a piece of candy from the coffee table, said good-bye and left.

Yuan was a very complex individual, in good spirits most of the time, but sometimes rather what I would say, "moody". In his words all he wanted to do was to paint, but he was cognizant of the fact that he also had to earn a living.

When he lived on Alta Avenue in Carmel, he would store his "finished" paintings under the house because he was dissatisfied with them. Nancy Johnson told us once, when we were in her gallery in Carmel, that if she could get him to give her these paintings, she could sell them for a great deal of money, but this he would not allow as he thought they were "no good."

He said that he could paint cypress tree after cypress tree, which he could do very quickly, to be sold in the art galleries, as this is what the gallery owners told him tourists would buy, but this he would not do. He wanted to paint what he wanted to paint.

I would run into him from time to time all over the Peninsula wearing that bulky knitted sweater, I remember so well, either painting or just standing or sitting, gazing off into space, and could not engage him in a conversation. All he would do is say "hello" and that's all.

The last time I saw him was in August, 1974. He had asked us to come visit him as he was having personal problems. He was in his "new home" located, I believe, in High Meadows in Carmel. He had a partially completed painting on an easel which he said

88. EVENING CLOUDS
Oil on canvas
12" x 16"

he could not finish as he was no longer able to paint. Also he showed us the interior of his double garage which contained row after row of paintings. He seemed to be terribly depressed. He wanted us to find him a small house in Carmel Valley. We tried to comfort him but to no avail. Unfortunately we were leaving the next day, to be gone three weeks, but we told him we would see him immediately upon our return. When we returned home from our trip, our son had left the obituary notice on our dining room table. Such a sad day. ☞

33. LOOKOUT GATE
Oil on board
22 1/2" x 32"

38. SAN MIGUEL DE ALLENDE
    Oil on canvas
    24" x 30"

34. UNTITLED
     Oil on masonite
     30" x 40"

2.   UNTITLED
     Oil on paper
     24" x 24"

1. CONWAY SUMMIT #2
   Oil on canvas
   10" x 36"

45. BLACKSMITH SHOEING HORSE
    Oil on masonite
    16" x 13"

Walter Georis

Yuan at work

46. PORTRAIT OF WALTER GEORIS
Conte crayon on paper
16" x 13"

WALTER GEORIS

Born in Belgium, photographer, painter, restaurateur and vintner, Walter Georis was a friend and student of S. C. Yuan in the early 1970s.

From an interview in May, 1993.

When I moved here in 1970, I opened a photography studio in the Doud Arcade. One day I had this visit from this guy. I didn't know who he actually was. He just started talking. At the time I was in Keith's drawing class. So I met Keith [Lindberg] and Reed [Farrington] and Yuan separately. He used to come to the studio two or three times a week. I was strictly doing photos at that time, drawing some at the classes, but Yuan didn't know I did that.

He kind of liked me, I guess. I think it ties in with the fact that he wanted to go to France and paint. He wanted to go to Avignon. He actually invited me. He said, "Maybe you'd like to go with me." I said, "Oh sure". This was about six months later, and I had found out the painter he was. While I was doing the drawing, for about a year before I actually painted, we developed our relationship. We used to go to the Bistro and have cappucino, and talk, spend a lot of time.

As you know he always wore the same thing. Always had a pair of jeans, a blue sweater or a green sweater. That's all he wore, with a white shirt underneath.

We would spend a lot of time talking together, a couple of hours almost every day at one point. Then I started painting, and he began inviting me to go paint with him, which was really nice. I went twice, and it was disastrous. There was no way I could keep up with him. He was quick at what he was doing, and accurate. But, anyway, we went to a couple of places. He started coming over to the house after that.

That was when I was with Quincy. He would come several times a week to the house, and we would talk. I got bold enough to ask for criticism on a painting. He asked me, "You sure you want to know?" I said, "Yes." It was a little still life of peaches. I still have that painting. I've kept it because of that. He said, "You know the only problem with that painting? There's no juice." I said, "What do you mean, no juice?" "There's no juice in the fruit." I'll never forget that. That's all he said about the painting.

On occasion, when I felt really good about a painting, I would have the guts to ask him. He would just totally destroy the painting. I remember one of them, he said, "Yeah, very interesting. But you should cut the painting." I said, "What do you mean, cut?" He said, "Well, this part's good. You should cut and not be afraid. Just because its stretched, doesn't mean it has to stay stretched. You take this part, cut that part of the painting out, and that's your painting. Throw the rest away." In that way, he really encouraged a lot of experimenting which he was very good at. He would see other people's work and experiment immediately, copy or do mix media things, which I thought was one of his best qualities, including the spontaneity.

We all partook, also in the frustration, I won't say deterioration of his person, not at all, but he had a temperament that was really up and down. He would get really depressed, and get really high. I had met him just after he'd gone through buying those fancy sports cars. Apparently, he'd bought a Porsche.

I think I might have met Rae before her father, because my next–door neighbor had a daughter, who was about seven or eight years younger than I at the time, in high school, and she would pass by the studio with Rae. I don't know if Yuan came by because Rae knew me and said, "Oh there's this guy from Europe that's doing photography."

66. BLUE VASE
Oil on canvas
24" x 20"

53. SPANISH STREET
Oil on board
7 1/2" x 9 1/2"

As we developed more and more of a stronger relationship, I found myself between him and Mrs. Yuan and Rae. It's inevitable that you get involved with the problems that the people have. I would quite often spend time with Mrs. Yuan at the restaurant.

One day he decided to move out of her house because they were going to go through with the divorce. I said, "Yuan, you can always stay here if you like." I had a room. He said, " No, only if I can rent the room." I said, "Yuan I don't want to rent to you; you just come." He said, "No," and brought me a check. Somewhere in my files, I still have the check that he wrote and that I never cashed, for $175 for the room. He never spent the night however. He never did. But he'd brought over all of his paintings, and put them in my back yard. It was full of paintings. It was raining that day. The paintings were there three or four days. He moved them around, but he was always doing that.

I remember that he was constantly trying to break some rules. He felt it necessary, in order to be a little bit mad at painting or bitter. He needed to be somewhat bitter in order to create the excitement or the stimulus that sometimes the city offers, that Carmel didn't offer. He would try to prove that a painter doesn't need a studio. Even though he had quite an elaborate studio, he went on the road and painted a one man show, out of that big, old, yellow station wagon. I remember being in the parking lot of the Merry Peach restaurant, by Albertson's. He showed me the one–man show that he had put together. You could still see some of the paint on the tires from his going over a canvas, as he leaned it against the tire. He'd gone up to Montana, somewhere up there, in the mountains where there was snow. A lot of the paintings were of that subject.

It was at that time that I was introduced to his concept of the hens and chicken. Maybe, the egg and the chicken and I forget what it was. But sometimes the copies are better than the originals. So he would do maybe ten of the same painting, in different dimensions. In fact, he was right, some of the copies were better than the original. He was very good at copying himself. That was kind of fun to see.

I went four times to do some paintings with him. Two of the times I actually painted with him, and the other times I just happened to spend time with him. One of the times was a place called Fraidy's Court which was on Mission, with that little shopping area, across from Katy's restaurant. They still had the little old houses there. There was a garage sale that day, so he decided to paint the garage sale. It was probably a 30" x 30" canvas, and if I remember correctly, it was burlap. He would use white glue, and then put some gesso over it, then paint on it, because it had the texture.

He'd just lean the canvas up against the wall. He had his orange crate, where he kept his stuff. He would paint, and every ten or fifteen minutes he would step back. The wind would catch the canvas, and it would go in the dirt. He would lean it back up and continue painting. The dirt didn't bother him at all, because that was part of the texture, part of the effect that he was trying to achieve, it was part of his signature. He was very clever at that. He actually developed quite a reputation for all these things that are not common practice. And the painting as usual turned out really quite fabulous.

Another time was at the light by the airport in Monterey. Across the street there were a lot of dead trees. I said, " O.K., I'll meet you over there." By the time I got there, half his painting was finished. So I got my stuff out, but said, "Yuan, I can't start painting now, you're done and going to take off and I'm going to be standing here by myself." I don't remember the painting, but he'd gone through that relatively fast.

At Sunset Center, another time, he did a painting of a girl with a straw hat and a flute. That painting was a large painting, a beautiful painting, in pastel colors and with his grays and mauves. I think that time it was he, Keith, Reed and I painting that day at Sunset Center in an actual studio.

I went several times to his studio at the house and watched him paint. I remember him pointing at piles of drawings, how quickly he worked with drawings, and saying, "Well, that's for Rae." I'd

Painting on location

70. VIEW OF MONTEREY BAY
Oil on wood panel
35 1/2" x 47 1/2"

50. COASTAL CYPRESS
   Oil on masonite
   18" x 14"

say, "What do you mean?" He said, "She'll never have to work. She can, whenever she needs some money, just sell one of the drawings." And in fact, it's true.

He did destroy a significant number of paintings that he felt weren't quite up to par, things that lay around the yard, that people would love to have now. Not that they were particularly good paintings, but they would be instrumental in showing what the process was, unfinished paintings, or partially treated surfaces that were prepared for a painting.

He was also very well known for painting over paintings. He would paint over some nice paintings, paintings typical of his work. I picked up that same habit. You become lazy sometimes, and don't want to stretch canvas, and you've got a painting you're not too crazy about. You scrape off what you can. That's one of the traits I picked up from him, plus the mud.

When he cleaned his brushes, the pigment all went to the bottom and he got that mud color. That was probably his most important paint. Everything was mixed with that to get those muted colors. He would take some of that, mix it in, and that would tie all the colors together. He would do his initial layout with that, or with a little darker paint. He would usually take the paint brush, and draw on the canvas. He would use oil or acrylic, and with a Chinese loose brush, break up the space. Then he would start filling it in with the paint, and let that initial drawing cut through here and there, forming a black line around the edge of something in a lighter color. That gave it that sculpted look, that feeling you get that the paintings were cut out.

He would check by, he would come down to the house, and to Keith's. He would do a circle of his friends. He would leave notes at the house, and I still have one of the rocks from the beach, where it says, "Everything satisfactory. The Inspector." And I still have that rock.

I remember him being invited down to Keith's house, one night for a steak, filet mignon. We were all sitting there saying, "When is Yuan going to show up?" We went to check if the front door were open or not, and we saw a note. He'd left a steak. I think he'd brought his own steak or something like that. He'd come up to the door and didn't want to be social. I don't think he was good at being social in a group situation. One to one he was fine. He could express himself and his frustrations, and his excitement over things.

He told me of an event that happened to him as a young man, or maybe as a child, during the war between the Chinese and Japanese. He told me he had gone into a temple to hide out. There was a mother, breast feeding her child, and part of her body had been blown off, or her head had been cut off, some really awful experience. It was something that stayed with him his whole life.

I remember having a little display at King of Hearts, some copper plates, suspended. I put some onions and shallots on one as a display and they had sprouted. He came to buy that. He said, "If I can get the onions with it, I'll buy the plate." It was a still life to him. So I said to him, "Yuan, you can just borrow it." "No, no, I want to buy it from you." He never wanted to be financially obligated. It was an expensive plate at that time, and I said, "No you can just take it." But he said "No," and bought the plate and took off with the onions and did a painting. He was always looking for material, so whenever he would see something that would work, he would either take it back to the studio or bring the studio to it.

When he did his last one–man show, I also had a one–man show at the same time. I had the small room, he had the big room at the Carmel Art Association. I was there that night. I don't remember if he'd said it to me or if I heard it, but he said he wasn't going to be taking the show down. As a matter of fact, at the last minute he wasn't even sure if he wanted to do the show. I think, to put the show together, he'd done some paintings, but in order to give continuity, he had put copal medium all over the paintings. They were the shiniest paintings of Yuan's, I'd ever seen. People said, "Oh look how bright they are." I think the brightness

109. SUNBATHERS
Oil on canvas
18" x 24"

came from the copal medium. The whole place smelled like it, but it looked like a one–man show, because of the same finish on all the paintings.

I used to go often to the new house that they'd built up at Jack's Peak. He was proud of the steps that he'd designed. They were actually stepping stones. He had taken some rocks and cast them in concrete. I think they are still there.   So in some ways, they are little mini sculptures of Yuan's and have, besides an aesthetic value, a collector's value. I don't think anyone knows they're really there. Whenever I've gone there, I always look for them.

When I heard about it, the first person who called me was Inga from the store nearby. She called me and said, "Did you read the paper." I said, "No". She said, "Yuan committed suicide." The first thing I did, it just gives me chills even talking about it, even this far, even as long ago, was go over to the Art Association and wait for it to open up.   I was on the bench there, and I was crying, pissed off. I was really upset, as a friend, a close friend and as a student.   I have been fortunate in my life. I've had three masters.   I've had one in wine, one in photography and Yuan was my master in painting.   My first reaction was that he played a trick on me. I felt that selfish, and that I should have partaken in his death, on a philosophical level. I was really upset with him.

I, as well as a lot of people, ended up cutting little pieces of bougainvillea. I brought in a little piece, a twig, of bougainvillea stuck it on one of the paintings.   It took a long, long time to get used to the fact that he wasn't here. It was just so painful for me. I cried and cried and cried, my God.

I went to the funeral.   I think I was one of the few people because nobody was invited.   Mrs. Yuan had said, " I know you were close, and if you'd like to come to the service, you know it'll be in Pacific Grove."   I went, but I couldn't go inside. I was crying outside, really upset. He'd been cremated.

72. UNTITLED
Watercolor on paper
20 1/2" x 27 1/2"

I can go back and talk about some of the little things. The art dealer, Les Laky was a very big part of commercialization of Yuan's paintings. It's through Les that I bought a lot of paintings when Yuan was in that gallery. Les was very nice to me, and I was next door at our shop. I would go in there, and he would say, "Well look at this one." The paintings were $150-$200 at that time. That was a lot of money for me, because that was my house payment. But whenever I could, I'd go in there and buy a painting. I bought probably ten to twelve paintings. I still have some of them.

At that time of Yuan's death, my brother was in Paris and he had a bit more cash. I said, "Gaston, this is what happened. I think you should buy one of the paintings." It was a $1200 painting, and I got it for him. It was one of the trees, with Carmel beach behind it. He still has it. So in our family, we have one from the show, the last one–man show.

I have two portraits that he did of me. One is a little sketch, done while I was drawing. I didn't realize he was drawing me. It's in pen and felt pen. The other one is conte, a little bit more realistic and on the back it says, "Avec appréciation". The reason why he did that was kind of a thank you. Because I'd done a series of photos of him painting, black and white photos, maybe even a couple of color photos. I gave him about twenty pictures, different shots of him painting. It was on his birthday. I forget how old he was, but he said, "Nobody has ever given me anything for my birthday. It's the first time I've ever gotten anything for my birthday." That's why he did the portrait of me. It was drawn in five or ten minutes at Sunset Center, one night. He'd said, "Oh, just sit there." I had my arms crossed, a big mustache at that time and the longer hair. I was pretty excited that he'd given it to me.

We were very close and I think we both kind of clicked into the role that was necessary. We gave identity to each other. He was able to be the teacher and I was able to be the student and which gave meaning to both of us. ☞

59. HORSES
Oil on canvas
7 1/2" x 31 3/4"

86. CASTROVILLE #2
Oil on canvas
24" x 36"

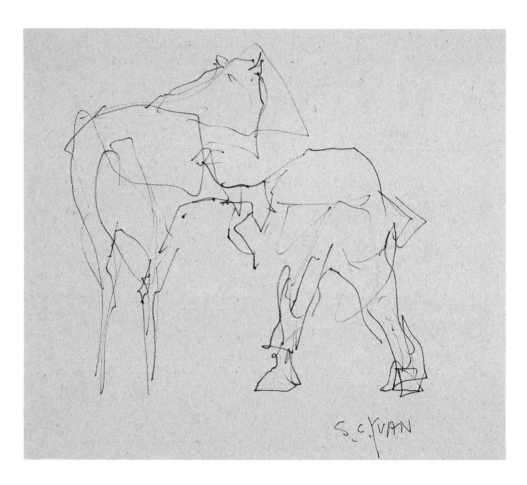

20. HORSE AND FIGURE #2
    Ink and chalk on paper
    8" x 8"

22. SEATED FIGURE #3
     Ink on paper
     10" x 8 1/2"

110. ON A BLUE PLATE
     Oil on panel
     12" x 16"

78. WINTER, SPAIN
   Oil on board
   26" x 31"

101. MONTEREY WHARF
Oil on masonite
12" x 16"

DELORES KALLER

Mrs. Kaller and her husband Robert owned Galerie de Tours in Carmel, and met S. C. Yuan through their gallery.

From an interview in March, 1994.

I met Yuan in the early sixties. We carried his work at the Galerie de Tours on Lincoln Street. There were only two galleries in Carmel when the Galerie de Tours opened in late 1959. Aside from the Smithson Gallery on the corner of Monte Verde and Ocean, there was the Carmel Art Association. So newcomers found it difficult to find a place to show their work. They hung their work in shoe stores and restaurants, wherever they could. Bob Kaller decided that the town needed another gallery, so he opened one. He was right. He was in the right place at the right time.

I started there in May of 1960. We carried a lot of the early artists like Harold and Mabel Landaker, S.C. Yuan and Joe Feuerborn. Yuan was so special. We were very pleased to have his work. He had a personality that was just electric. He'd come in, looking as if he'd been doing Tai Chi. He posed when he came in. He was fabulous. When he brought in new paintings, he would come bouncing up the stairs with a new story and visit with us, telling us about his life, what he was doing and talk about his sweet little daughter, Rae. It was really all a lot of fun.

As a newcomer to the area, Yuan's paintings seemed to me, to be similiar to Armin Hansen's. Simply because he used that palette, that beautiful blue-green grey, very rich, very subtle, with lots and lots of color. I have one of his paintings. It's of Monterey wharf, and is typical of his work, the blue–green, wonderful water.

Yuan the photographer

I love the texture. It's done with palette knife, very dimensional. You see the light and shadow of the surface, caused by the depth of the paint.

He loved to cook. I think cooking was almost more of a passion than the painting. And eventually he opened that restaurant called the Merry Peach, which was in the Carmel Rancho area.

Yuan was with us for three or four years. We got along with him, even though he had a volatile temperament, because I think Mr. Kaller understood him and could empathize with him. He could see the spark of genius there. He was always so into his work, so alive. It's amazing to me that he ended the way he did. Quite frankly, it was a great shock to all of us. I do remember him fondly and wish he were still with us. ✑

91. HUNTER'S POINT
Oil on board
10" x 23"

54. MEETING
   Oil on board
   7 1/2" x 9 1/2"

69. VILLAGE STREET SCENE
   Oil on canvas,
   8" x 11"

Claudia Peterson and Yuan at Petersons' picnic

25. WINTER, PARIS
Oil on board
16" x 20"

CLAUDIA PETERSON

Born in France, met S. C. Yuan through Yuan's brother, John, in the mid–1960s.

From a letter written in March, 1994.

I met S.C. Yuan through his brother, John Yuan, for whom I worked in 1964 and 1965, taking care of John's frame shop, Forest Hill Frames, on Forest Avenue in Pacific Grove . This venture was to help him and his artist friends in acquiring reasonably priced frames for their works.

S. C. would come occasionally and work on the frames himself, when his brother was teaching Mandarin at the Defense Language Institute. And then he'd sit and we'd talk, mainly about Paris or other cities and countries, about color, always ending by saying he had plans and I was to feature in them. Awed by his friendship, I never asked what they were nor what my role would be in them. He also would come by the house, in Ft. Ord, for a cup of French coffee (in those days, the now ubiquitous espresso bar was non–existant) and a few cookies. Sometimes he would bring a birthday cake or a welcome home one, if it was the occasion or if we had been gone on a holiday. He commented on the pure lines of my French drip coffee pot (cafetiére Salam) as if it were some exotic object! Sometimes he would talk politics, if my husband was home. He never wanted to bring into the conversation memories of China and he told me he never wanted to go back there nor to Taiwan. He seemed very bitter, often angry at life, at the mediocrity of every day living. He still had ambitions, and wanted fortune, not as money to invest for the future, but as a means to satisfy quickly a desire or a whim like a flashy car or a trip abroad. He loved to travel, preferably in the fall, and found pleasure in Spain and some parts of Italy, where the rather somber, earthy colors could respond to his own palette. He dismissed French country side as being much too green! But he liked Paris for its history and art emanating from all its pores. He liked the old parts of the city, the village feeling of each neighborhood, the narrow streets and brown buildings, the stops at the café terraces becoming interminable stays, with long, drawn–out conversations or solitary comtemplations, meditations.

We had a lovely picnic once, provided by him, at Point Lobos, with my husband and four children. Michelle, five at the time, remembers it as feeling "European!" (I think she meant worldly or exotic, relaxed and exciting). S. C. did some sketches of Linda, fourteen, sitting on a rock, which became a lovely little painting we named, *The Little Mermaid*, and which was bought by a doctor, I believe. Linda went two other times with her guitar to pose for him in his Carmel studio and was so excited to have earned money for it! She found him "humorous," joking with her to relieve the tension and make it easier to pose for a long stretch at a time, another facet of his normally serious comportment. We also met his wife and daughter at another get–together.

He liked my father's paintings and even framed some himself to show them for awhile in his second gallery. They did not sell, but I still have the frames, the only "art" of S. C. that I own, never having asked for, nor bought a memento.

Looking back on his many visits, I am filled with regret at having been so naive and a little afraid of this great artist who befriended me, as I did not always understand what he was mumbling about and did not ask questions. I was a listener if he wanted to talk or let off steam (literally sometimes, after having to work in the kitchen of his wife's restaurant) or merely a provider of a place to sit silently and enjoy a cup of coffee as in a Paris bistro. ✎

47. WOMAN IN CHAIR
Oil on board
16" x 20"

40. HORSES
    Ink on paper
    4 1/2" x 10"

23. FIGURE BENDING OVER
Ink and chalk on paper
10" x 8 1/2"

On the Spanish Steps, Rome

58. SICILY
Oil pastel on paper
13 1/2" x 18 1/2"

GERALD WASSERMAN

Carmel Art Association member, painter and sculptor, Gerry Wasserman was dividing his time between Carmel and Italy, in the early 1970s.

From an interview in February, 1993.

I was in Rome. Yuan and I hardly knew each other, other than in passing. I got a letter "Dear Gerry, it will be great to see you, etc." like old pals, "I'll see you soon." Before I had time to answer the letter, it was about 8:15 to 8:30 one morning, and I had overslept. You needed an elevator key to get off of it on our floor. I heard the buzzer, and I thought it was the intercom downstairs. It was Yuan at my elevator door. I called through and said, "I'm not dressed, but come in". He was ALL excited about painting in Rome. Two days later we saw each other again, and Yuan said, "I think I'm going to Sicily." He hadn't seen Rome. He left Rome. Then he came back from Sicily and had done about twenty paintings and he had gotten a locker at the airport and stored his brushes and paints there and just left them. He never did return to get his supplies. Yuan asked me later that year, when I was having my Carmel Art Association show, when I would return to Rome, and if I would go to the airport, I could have his things.

Rome was where we got to know each other. He was staying at a nice fancy hotel. He had a room at the Andrea Doria Hotel. Invited us to dinner. We went to the concierge because he was not downstairs. They seated us in the dining room. My wife and I had gotten dressed up, and down the stairs he swept into the room with a nice clean shirt, and blue jeans covered in paint. The whole room was staring at this bohemian Chinese American! I thought he was showing he was a painter. It was not like he had a few spots of paint, those were his painting pants!

Once, while I was having an opening at the Carmel Art Association, Yuan came and asked, "Who is making pictures (photographs)?" Yuan was very generous and also acted brusque, like he did not care. Yuan asked about the pictures, and I explained that sometimes the *Herald* would come and take pictures. Yuan said, "No, no they will not come, I'll make the pictures." He left and came back and took very good pictures. He said to come to his restaurant the next morning, bring the announcement of the show, double-spaced and typed, and the photographs would be ready for me to take to the *Herald*.

After the opening when everyone was leaving, I saw a red dot (meaning sold) that I didn't know anything about on a painting. I asked, and was told Yuan had said, "Save that one for me."

One time, when I was talking to Yuan before he left on another trip to Europe, I asked him, "You go over to do some painting because you like those subjects?" Yuan said, "You can paint anywhere, I can paint anywhere, I don't go over there for those subjects, I go over there because the people like those subjects."

After he returned, I saw him and asked him, "You brought back the work you did on the trip? You are going to have a show of the work now?" Yuan said, "You show the chicken?" I said, "What?" Yuan said, "You show the chicken? I don't sell the chicken, I show the eggs. I keep the chicken for my children. I sell the eggs." He did not explain. I later found out he made copies of his originals or slightly different versions, but very, very close, without losing quality; not what you expect in a copy. He could do that, most artists cannot.

When he hung his last show, I was at the gallery, and I said the show looks good. He said, "I'm putting it up but not taking it down." He told me that, this had been rattling around a long time. My wife was ill at the same time. He called me to see if I could come see his new house.

Of course I did not realize his mental condition at the time. He said, "Here I have all this, and I don't give a damn about it." He said, "I have nothing anymore." He deprecated certain paintings, of others he said, "That's pretty good", then he deprecated more. That was the last time I saw him. ✐

96. UNTITLED
Oil on board
8" x 10"

80. SEASCAPE
Oil on board
12" x 24"

31. CARMEL
    Oil on canvas
    30" x 36"

105. PINE TRE
Oil on can
36" x 60 1/
Exhibited
last show a
Art Associ
September

26. CYPRESS
Oil on board
12" x 16"

towel, and he would just do a little thumbnail, a little sketch to illustrate. Very brief in terms of words, he would try to give me what I wasn't seeing, or what I needed to see, just by doing it next to me like that. It was wonderful. It was very magical because it was almost like a little silent blessing; that he walked by and checked what I was doing.

One evening he had done a little thumbnail, and we took a break. I was sitting on one of the tables, just sitting there drinking something, and he came and sat down next to me. Again, he would almost never look directly at me, and he started talking. Talking about his wife and how sad he was, he broke into tears. I was so touched and I felt so badly for him that I had tears streaming down my face. When he finally turned around to look at me, he said, "Oh my God, you are crying with me". He was so touched, and that's how we became friends, and from then on we were very close friends.

I started helping him out, and I would talk to him, because he was very depressed about his wife. The big thing at that time was that he couldn't work, he was not able to paint. He had built a new house for her, and it was very sad for him, because he was going to be moving into that house without her.

He kind of went into a rage of cleaning out old things. I was helping him clean out his house, the old house. He built a huge fire in the backyard. We would be in the garage which was completely strewn with paintings, drawings, I mean unframed, framed, in every condition possible, with prints all over, and he would start saying, "You like this?" I said, "Yuan I really don't know. I'm not really trained". Well, I would say something like that, and he would throw it in the fire. I would say, "My God, Yuan this is too big of a responsibility, you should never ask me. I don't really know enough to tell you anything. You look at something and you decide. I can't do that".

Anyway at one point he pulled out an Armin Hansen. I was not familiar at that point with Hansen. I was like a babe in the woods. I really didn't have much training. I had a little bit of classical

98. THREE ORANGES AND PEARS
Oil on board
16" x 20"

background in painting, but I didn't know the local artists and what was happening on the scene. So he pulled it out and he looked at it and he said, "Armin Hansen". I didn't know who he was. He said, "$10,000 dollars for this painting. Do you believe that?", and he took it and threw it into the fire! I about died. I only realized afterward what he had done, and whose painting it was. Every time I think about it now, I just cringe. He loved Armin Hansen's work. I think he knew him.

We found all kinds of things in that house and garage that he had lost. One of the things that I came across was his little stamp (chop) which apparently he had not been able to find for several years. So when I found it, he gave out a yell, threw his arms around me and gave me a great big hug. He said, "I looked for this for years, and you find it." He kept it. He put it aside but I don't know what eventually happened to it. I could see that was such a personal thing to him. It meant a lot to him.

He did set up his studio in the new house and painted there. In fact he wanted to start painting again. I was trying to convince him to do that, and he asked if I would be his model. He had a vision and was getting very excited about working again. I thought if I could just help him to work, that's all I would want. It would make him so happy. He actually started on one painting. He got started on it, decided to take a break, and asked me to come over and take a look at it. Well, I should never have done that, because then he asked me what I thought of it. I said, "Well, it doesn't look much like me." You know, I was young and kind of egotistical about the painting. I wanted to look good in the painting, and I didn't look particularly anything. It was mostly shape and form and unfinished. Immediately I regretted not having been totally positive, because he never finished that painting.

It was at that point that we kind of cut things off, because he was just too vulnerable. I didn't want to carry the responsibility for someone's life, and he was ready to hand it over to someone. I was not in the position to do that. Not at all. It was not the right thing for me to do.

57. SNOW, SIERRA
Mixed media on canvas
60" x 30"

The other thing he wanted to do was teach me to paint. He said, "I can teach you how to do technical paintings, real quick. You can get established with that and then on the side you work doing abstracts. I teach you. You'll be a very good painter". So he had this plan for me; he was going to do this for me. I couldn't take up on it, because it was unfair to him in his position, for me to do that. I could see it would have gone wrong. I just told him that I thought it best if we probably didn't see each other too much.

And that's the way that went. It's a sad story. I had a sense that there was nothing I could do that would prevent the outcome. I would have been a bandaid on a big wound, and I didn't want any part of his death. I would have liked to have been a part of his painting and a part of his life, but I sensed that that was not going to be possible. He talked so much about honor, and how dishonored he was by Mrs. Yuan's leaving, and that that dishonor in China is a very big thing.

When we talked, we would have philosophical discussions. Often he would stop and look at me and say, "You talk like my daughter". Of course I did. I was young and immature. I was totally unripened and there were so many things I didn't understand. At the same time, though, I took the comment as a great compliment. I knew how much he admired his daughter, Rae. I really value the time I spent with him.

I remember a couple of stories he told me. He would tell me about his paintings , about how upset he used to get with people. He had a gallery at one time down on San Carlos near where the Red Lion used to be. He watched these people walking by. They went by just about every day, and he had put a painting up in the window. It was of cows. The people were talking about him, he could hear them from the inside. They loved the scene, but didn't quite approve of the cows, and thought that horses would be better. So the next day when they walked by, there were horses. He changed the cows into horses. He said, "See now they're horses, you can buy the painting!"

84. RAIN IN SPAIN
Oil on canvas
36" x 48"

104. SUNNY BAY
Oil on canvas
24" x 36"

Yuan docking in Europe

He would get so upset with people because they'd look at a painting, and say, "Well, I kind of like this part of the painting." One day he had some people who said that to him, and he took a pair of scissors or a knife and cut it, slashed it right where they liked it and he handed it over to them and said, "O.K.!"

And another story. He told me that he had sold a painting to some people. I don't know how much longer it was afterward, but there was something in his mind about that painting that needed changing. So he climbed in through the people's window and changed the painting on the wall. He told me that. I think they must have been away, but it bothered him so much, he went in, and made a couple of changes on the painting. I don't know if they ever noticed.

He was just so full of life and passion at sixty something. There was so much energy and so much creative vitality in that man. There is an abusiveness sometimes in that kind of character, because it can be, appear, brutal sometimes to people around them. He would follow these heat–of–the–moment impulses, and that is a very difficult place from which to operate. It is difficult on yourself and the people around you. I could see that Mrs. Yuan did not always have a very easy time. He had a very tender heart and was extremely sensitive. He had trouble reconciling the cultural differences of his heritage and living here. Communication broke down within himself. He would totally dedicate himself to the restaurant, and then flip to the other side, and become totally dedicated to painting. Very child–like, every moment passionate and impulsive.

I remember going over to his new house with Walter and Gaston, when it was completed, but not quite finished inside. He had polished cement floors that had paint in them. It was a real different look. Highly polished, they actually looked really beautiful. The room was completely empty except for a couple of items, stacks of paintings and so forth, and one of those tall, free standing stoves, Norwegian. The room had a very tall ceiling. It went up real high, and the room echoed. At one point in talking to us, he broke into song. It was "Old Man River". When he came

102. STILL LIFE WITH RED ROSE
Oil on masonite
8" x 10"

67. THE GINZA, RAINY DAY IN TOKYO
Oil on burlap
36" x 48"

Sam Harris

Yuan painting in Su Vecino Court

17. MEDITERRANEAN MARKET
Oil on board
12" x 16"

SAM HARRIS

Carmel Art Association member, painter, living in Carmel and Italy, Sam Harris knew S. C. Yuan in the 1960s and early 1970s.

From an interview in January, 1994.

I'm not sure of the date but it must have been thirty to thirty–two years ago when I first met Yuan. I was living in Monterey at the time, and had my studio there. A group of us got together and hired a model. Yuan came over one day. About half way through the afternoon, we changed the model's pose. Tried another angle. I wasn't too happy with what we had, so I asked her to change the pose. He picked up his stuff and left without saying a word!

He had a restaurant on Cannery Row and did some of the cooking there. He asked me if I would like to come in with him and have a frame store. I thought it was kind of a good idea, so I talked to Steve Crouch. He said, "Oh no, Sam. Don't get involved with Yuan, he's a very difficult person." So I kind of gave up on that idea!

Then later, probably twenty–seven years ago, I came back from Europe with my wife and decided to have a little gallery in Carmel and sell my paintings. So I found a place in Su Vecino Court, a little gallery upstairs. Yuan had another gallery on the second floor, much larger, with nice carpeting and lighting. I got to know him a little better there. In fact, one time I saw him painting downstairs in the courtyard. He had a couple of young teenagers posing for him. So I rushed out and took some photographs of him. I tried not to bother him, but I thought he'd make a nice subject to paint. I never got around to doing the paintings until recently.

29. MARBELLA, SPAIN
    Oil on canvas
    26" x 31"

77. PARIS
    Oil on board
    20" x 30"

Y. S. LIM

Born in China, Carmel Art Association member, painter and collector, Y. S. Lim became friends with S. C. Yuan after meeting him in the early 1960s.

From stories written by Y. S. Lim in April, 1994.

This beautiful, pine painting [*Twin Pine*] was in his last one–man show at the Carmel Art Association. Three days after he hung his show, he passed away. When the news of his death spread, I was one of many who went to the gallery to view his show and pay our respects to one of our best, to collect our thoughts and memories, each in our own little way, recounting any event at all.

Selling paintings was a concern of Yuan's. It weighed heavily during our conversations when he visited my gallery. Selling his paintings was essential to him. I think he needed that emotional high to kick off his new day.

For three consecutive days, I visited his show. As I stared at the price list posted on the wall, not a single star (indication of sold) was on that list! The visitors to his show were too busy telling of their encounters with Yuan and had forgotten what is important to an artist's one–man show. Put your money where the mouth is and let it speak silently, but loud and clear, of how much you like his work. The star–less price list had saddened me deeper than the news of his death. His death was expected. We had talked about this into the early hours of the morning, during his troubled times. His conviction was to die at the age of sixty–three, because his father died at that age.

12. TWIN PINES
Oil on canvas
60" x 40"

unexpected goal; why paint with muted color when you already know what it can do. Get off your safety net and try some colors that you never thought of using. Your muted color is well known. You should throw people a curve, by painting bright, and smiling at them, and let them wonder why. His last one-man show certainly was the most colorful one that we all remember. I think people were caught by surprise, and in wondering why, forgot to buy.

Though I had put my star on *Twin Pine* to indicate it was sold, it was still just a lone star on the price list. I guess the brighter color still did not help his sales. I started to feel cynical when someone came up to me and told me how beautiful the colors on Yuan's new paintings were. In fact I was mad enough to over-draft our account to put the second star on the price list. If that did not start up the sales, I was planning to get a loan to buy the whole show, as I had done before to buy his paintings. That's how I got a large collection of Yuan paintings.

I returned two days after I had put my second star on *Red Bouga-invillea*, to check the price list. Boy, what a difference two days made! Aside from my pen drawing of two stars, most of the paint-ings had a red dot next to them. I was told the whole show was bought up by local artists. What a way to go, Yuan! My one regret is Yuan didn't give encores. Why did you have to go in such a hurry? I found great joy with your *Red Bougainvillea*. I wish you the same wherever you may be.

Slowly but surely, we were collecting Yuan's work, from his home studio. The *Snow Sierra* was one of his "chicken" paintings, or not for sale. The more it was not for sale, the more we wanted it. We haggled for months, until he finally named a price. I couldn't refuse. It was three times higher than other chickens I managed to get from him. So I went away with *Snow Sierra* in my hand and our savings account in his pocket.

A few months later, he wanted to know if he could buy back *Snow Sierra*. Deep down, and to be fair to my colleague, I felt I should

8. SNOW SIERRA
   Oil on canvas
   36" x 60"

sell it back because it was the pride of his work. I told him I would loan it back to him on a Chinese five–year plan. He never took up on it. Later he asked for the loan of this painting for his last one-man show at the Pacific Grove Art Center. He had plenty of paintings, and I had seen how he could finish three paintings in one morning. He did not need this painting for the show, unless it were one of his all time favorites.

One early morning, when I went out to get our newspaper, I found this painting (*Potted Flower with Long Black Tray*), against the wall, just outside the front door. It took the sleepy eye out of me. As I turned the painting over, I discovered it was one of Yuan's. Why is it here? What's the occasion? When was Yuan here? How did he know that it was our wedding anniversary? With grace, we accepted his kindness and generosity, and oh, what fun for me to be Charlie Chan's #1 son, just for one morning. I never found out any answers to the questions. Who cares, as long as we know Yuan is Santa Claus in disguise. If one sees within, one may find there is no need to question, hence need no answer.

11. POTTED FLOWER WITH LONG
    BLACK TRAY
    Oil on board
    16" x 20"

One morning, Yuan showed up in his station wagon. It was full of painting materials and he wanted to paint my lily pond. But when he saw my wife, Irene, she was knitting in the garden where the water lilies were. He made her a proposition she could not refuse. If she would let him paint her knitting, the first painting would be for her to keep, the second painting for him. First, he did a most beautiful drawing on this canvas with bristle brush and acrylic. It was so beautiful, I could have cried, don't paint over it, but didn't, not wanting to upset his painting mood. It was painful to watch this beautiful, Chinese–brush–stroke drawing, being painted out. So I went away to water my other garden, instead of watching in pain and in silence. I returned half an hour later, but by then there was no drawing left.

13. IRENE KNITTING
    Oil on canvas
    30" x 40"

What was amazing to me was that as he painted, he moved and rearranged the umbrella on the canvas many times, with different

143

colors, positions and sizes. Within about thirty minutes, like there was nothing to it! He would ask me, "What do you think?" I did not think his questions were aimed directly at me, because there would go that umbrella, with another taking shape, with no sign of struggle, as far as application of paint was concerned. It amazed me that he could go on and on until he thought he got it.

When the second painting made its debut at the Carmel Art Association's monthly show, many people came to my gallery and told me how much they liked Yuan's painting. It was untitled then.

Again, what amazed me was, if I looked closely at Irene's face, there was no detail of eyes, nose or mouth. All one saw was a few brush strokes of light or dark in abstract shape, and yet there was no doubt that it was Irene. I thought, this painting will become my teacher. I cannot live without it. So I bought it from the Carmel Art Association.

———————

This painting [*Three Deer on the Snow*] holds a special feeling for me. Yuan had given us a few paintings through the years, but *Three Deer on the Snow* was a gift from his widow, Jen–Chi Yuan, as a token of appreciation, shortly after his death. With these three deer, Yuan illustrated tenderness, loving, caring feelings, so delicately done, instead of his usual powerful brush strokes. The care–giving side of his temperament was rarely displayed in person, but it is so well brought out in this painting.

Early in the summer of 1970, he was at our home for one of his just-drop-in visits, to do some drawings of water lilies. He remarked that he could paint here for months, without setting foot outside of the garden gate. I could sense that now was the time to move in with the kill with kindness. I told him we were going to Hawaii. I invited him to use our house during our absence. I showed him where everything was, for whatever he needed, for two weeks. I even encouraged him to bring Jen–Chi and stay a while as a mini honeymoon. She could actually enjoy sun tanning

15. THREE DEER ON THE SNOW
    Watercolor on paper
    14" x 19"

until she needed to run back to Carmel and open their restaurant. He hung a smile on this face, but I know he was embarrassed. He accepted the spare house key. That was good.

When we returned we found that there were many outdoor chairs stacked up high in the garden. Some soul had ingeniously tried to protect a cake box from animals getting into it. It was a bakery– decorated, "Welcome Home," cake. We thought, it can't be Yuan's doing, because he didn't touch anything in the house nor studio nor guest house. Besides, a just-drop-by with a bag of donuts would suit him fine, and be more to his style. We happily settled for a cup of coffee and cake. There, inside the box, under the cake, was an envelope which held the keys to our house and to the mystery. I was deeply moved, because I knew deep down, way down, he had all the right stuff to be a caring, tenderhearted and gentle man. I was impressed by his action and learned a little more about why it is hard to be humble, when one knows one can be, if one wants to, perfect in every way.

––––––––––

The magnificent "Veteran Cypress" is still living at Point Lobos Reserve State Park. One day in 1969, Yuan came to my gallery, somewhat excited with pride. He wanted me to go with him to the Laky Gallery, which was three doors down, to look at the large painting he had just finished.

It was awesome for me to see such a major painting for the first time. I have never seen before or since an artist who could combine the East and West and make it shine and yet keep his roots intact. Yuan is known for his oils, but his way with the brush can only come from the hand of a master calligrapher. Every time I look at *Veteran Cypress*, I see less of the tree and more of the calligraphy. This is the strength and trademark of S. C. Yuan. ✐

18. VETERAN CYPRESS
Oil on canvas
60" x 80"

64. SWEET PEAS
   Oil on board
   20" x 16"

74. FOGGY MORNING
   Oil on canvas on masonite
   30" x 40"
   This painting was entered in the
   1959 Monterey County Fair under
   the pseudonym of "Zambini" (signed
   in the lower right corner), because
   Yuan felt the judges might be biased
   against his new style of painting.
   After winning a prize for this
   painting, he partially overpainted
   the pseudonym and added his usual
   signature in the upper right corner.

83.

Yuan painting in Su Vecino Court

42. BIRD ON A BRANCH
Oil on canvas
44" x 43 3/4"

ROLLIN PICKFORD

*Carmel Art Association member, painter, Rollin Pickford met
S. C. Yuan while spending the summer in Carmel in the late
1950s. He lives in Fresno.*

From a letter written in December, 1993.

Yuan was our next door neighbor one memorable summer in
Carmel. His daughter, Rae, became the playmate of our children.

We became good friends and painting companions. His generosity was boundless. He shared his delectable Chinese cooking
with us. He shared all his motifs with me, landscape, the sea,
still life, portrait sitters. I can remember painting portraits in
his home, in his restaurant, in his yard.

But, best of all, he shared his remarkable personality and his painting knowledge and insights.

"I show you whole new world of Oriental watercolor," he prom-
ised.

And he did.

When I was struggling with the image of a flock of gulls, "Two
birds are better than three," he would say, "One bird is best."

Sound advice.

Once when I had been painting on the mountain all day, I returned at evening and looked over the fence into his yard. The

entire area and patio were covered with watercolors of the bougainvillea on the side of our house.

"How did you do, Yuan?" I asked.

His reply was entirely characteristic. "All tragedies, all disasters," he moaned, raising his hands above his head.

Then he shuffled madly through the day's work and found one small area in one watercolor that he liked. He dipped a brush in water and outlined the area on the rice paper and pulled the image out. The rest of his production he wadded up and consigned to the incinerator. I watched covetously as it all went up in smoke.

Another philosophy of his: "Abstract is just close-up of something," he would say, pointing to a wood grain or the texture of seaweed or any other handy object.

After dinner our discussions ranged over religion, philosophy, art, literature. That summer he was reading Goethe's "Italian Journey."

At his passing, I felt a serious personal loss as well as a concern for what the community was denied—a fine intellect, deep passion, ultra sensitivity and those measured and fine paintings with their wise equilibrium. ☞

95. THREE BOATS
Oil on board
18" x 24"

93. SEASCAPE
Oil on masonite
8 1/2" x 23 3/8"

100. ARTICHOKE STAND
   Oil on board
   9" x 12"

35. UNTITLED
   Oil pastel and ink on paper
   24" x 18"

the south grounds of Sunset Cultural Center. Yuan did not like fat models, and when one of the models who was amply endowed modeled, Yuan just sat around and waited to go for coffee after class. Nights he would draw, he did 20 or 30 drawings. He was a quick man and liked the one minute poses. He would stand or sit on the floor, all the time squinting his eyes while looking at the model.

On the Tuesday before his death, he came to the house and asked when class was starting and said that he would be there. That evening he was so low and felt he would never make it out of the divorce. Yuan's divorce has been going on for 3 years now. The first time Mrs. Yuan moved out, he went and bought a gun and threatened to kill her and himself. She was afraid and came back home. From this time on, there was a gun around and he talked about ending himself often.

That night he was so low, he said he was looking for a dishwashing job. He asked, "Tell me the alternatives, what other jobs can I get." I said they need someone at Del Mesa to teach a painting class and that I would call and get it set up. He brightened up. I said he could also do demos at the art associations around California.

For the next few months in 1974, Keith Lindberg filled his journal pages with his memories of Yuan. The following are some excerpts.

I had met Yuan in 1964. Robert E. Lee III and his wife Amy had opened a gallery, 800 sq. ft., upstairs and across the street from Yuan's gallery on San Carlos at 7th, middle of the block, in the Vandervoort Court. Yuan came to see my work, like he did with every painter that came into the area. Amy was sitting the gallery and met Yuan first. She was excited that such a good painter would climb the stairs to see my work. She did not realize he looked at everyone new in the area. Yuan made short talks, like he always did. And said he liked some of the works. Yuan always liked talking to pretty young girls, and Amy was no exception, so he came back again. I met Yuan at the Lee's gallery. There was not much said and we went for coffee at the Craft Center. Not

92. HEAD #2
Pastel on paper
15" x 12"

Back in the 1950s, a friend that lived next door, leaned across the fence and asked, "Are you mixing up some more of that gravy, Yuan?" Yuan would say to me, " Color in a painting is like pouring tabasco sauce over one's dinner. Color ruins a painting."

He cared nothing for the materials on which he painted, or maybe he just seemed that way, for he would paint on any material. Cotton, he would size with white glue, then gesso it, and begin throwing washes and sometimes India ink over the canvas surface. If the design was to his satisfaction, he would continue to paint. Painting thin in the beginning. Mixing his paint in large areas with turp. Sometimes letting the paint dry for a day or so then maybe throwing ink over the surface again. At the end mixing thick paint with a palette knife and laying the paint on with care. He'd say never brush on paint. Place the paint on the canvas.

Yuan would squint when he painted and did drawings. He said when you squint it drops out all the middle values and one only sees the highlights and the dark darks.

He painted over many of his works, sometimes three, four, or five times. Each time scraping and sanding the canvas. Many times he would see things he liked in a canvas and just pick up where he left off, repainting the canvas, letting the under painting show through. Many of his works are now cracking and crazing. Yuan painted on canvas, masonite, plywood and jute. On masonite he would paint five boards then let them sit a couple of days. Taking a power saw, he would cut new compositions from the painting.

Yuan never liked his paintings. I think because he never believed the paintings were a reflection of himself. Maybe he felt himself to be an even better painter. After he painted them, his paintings were like children in his life and sometimes met with his child-like temper. He would walk on them or take a knife and cut the center from one. Yuan said he was treated badly by his father, and his paintings being his children, got no different treatment, than had his father's children. Bad treatment, I guess.

Sjef Wildschut

Painting in his studio on Alta Avenue

32. WEST COAST
Oil on masonite
30" x 40"

Yuan always painted two kinds of paintings. A chicken and an egg. He always repeated his paintings, subject and color and design. The chicken was the best painting, which he kept and copied. Using the chicken painting to produce his egg paintings, which were lesser, to be sold to the public, always keeping the chicken, to paint more eggs!

Though he was a purist at heart, and said that paintings should come from within the person, out on to the canvas, not from out to inside one, and then outside again, he would work from slides. He painted from colored slides a lot. When in Europe, he would not paint much, but would shoot 35mm slides to paint from back home. I would ask him if he had done some corny paintings. He would say no. He was always mad about the public's taste.

Yuan admired Delacroix, particularly, *Raft of the Medusa*, Daumier and early Picassos. His favorite painting of his own was, *The Pilgrimage*. A large group–type painting of figures, very close in value, about 6' x 8'. He asked $10,000 for the painting, but gave it to his wife.

Yuan very much admired his art professor in China, but said that his training with the professor was too academic. Yuan always talked of experimenting. He was always looking at other painters' work, for techniques. He did a lot of collage work with tissue paper.

Yuan was about line. Line in his work meant more than mass. Armin Hansen used line the same way. Yuan on seeing Hansen's work identified strongly with the line and muted color. I have heard it said, that Yuan used to sit in front of the White Oaks Gallery in Carmel Valley and study the Armin Hansen paintings in the window. Yuan's style is of two influences, his Chinese training and that of the paintings of Hansen. Armin Hansen paintings were dark, with the quick brush stroke, like Yuan's.

I feel he painted like one that was writing a letter. To him the most important part of painting, was the painting, the action of painting itself.

gallery there. He arrived, drove up in front of the gallery, got out and looked in the window. The gallery owner saw him and was coming out to greet him. Yuan turned from the window, got in his car and drove back to Carmel, never to contact the gallery again. He said the gallery didn't look good.

Once he even threatened to hit the art dealer, Les Laky, with a telephone, over a one–man show. Yuan always said he hated his work, and when shows were hung, he said, "Throw them to the public, the dumb people deserve such bad work."

Yuan used to say if you get mad at the treatment you get from the Carmel Art Association, sidestep them, but never get out. They can be petty, but they can't make you take out your paintings. And that's what he did, he kept his paintings on the walls at that gallery, in good times and bad.

Yuan had shown his work at Zantman's on and off since 1965. This last time, Yuan was happy with Zantman and felt that Zantman was really trying to help him. His last show there, the paintings were pure. He did not start with the subject. He started by throwing washes and letting things happen and using the happening to his advantage, making decisions about proportion in the first place. All the paintings came from within, and at the end the subject appeared; for he had a love and great feeling for things of this earth. At the big show at Zantman's, *Girl with the Red Shawl* was on the cover of the catalog.

This is a story about Yuan and a dealer. One good thing was that the dealer did not have good taste. This took place about five years ago. The dealer was a man who came up from Southern California about once a year and liked to make these trips, buying paintings. He always looked up a painter and went to the studio to make a deal. He always offered cash, in $100 bills, and was always trying to buy as cheap as possible. He would buy without frames, three or four at a time, he wanted fifty percent off, and he would push for sixty percent off. Not having good taste, he never took a painter's best pieces. He bought from Yuan, Wasserman and me. The last sale I made to him was for five 8" x 10"s for $50

Yuan painting in Su Vecino Court

14. GIRL AT THE SUNNY SHORE
Oil on canvas
32" x 48"

each, and they sold retail for $125 each. But I took the cash. One day, Yuan saw the dealer in front of the Carmel Art Association and said it was good to see him. Before the dealer could say anything, Yuan said that he was mad at a client. The client had promised to buy four paintings the day before at 3 p.m., and had not shown up at Yuan's studio as promised. Yuan told him, "You come to my studio, and I will sell the paintings of the client, for $50 each." The dealer jumped at the deal and showed at 3 p.m. He wanted to buy other paintings, but Yuan said no, only the four. Later that day, the dealer showed these to me, which he had in the trunk of his car. They were bad. Yuan had sold him three unfinished paintings and one small Paris scene. One was a donkey and cart, badly painted, but he said he'd gotten a great deal. Poor man.

To Yuan all his life, there were things for a man to do, things for a woman to do and things for Yuan to do. He would never carry the groceries into the house. Mrs. Yuan and Rae always did this chore. As a painter, I can only see this as good. Always thinking of painting is the only way to get a body of work together in one's lifetime. And he did this. I admit, it is hard on loved ones, being around this type of person, for they are expected to hold life together and live with the painter's selfish whims.

Yuan went out to buy needed groceries for the restaurant. He then went home to fix Mrs. Yuan her lunch. After lunch Mrs. Yuan would take a rest, and Yuan would go down to work in the restaurant until Mrs. Yuan came down. Yuan went home to paint in the afternoon. He said, then he might go down to help close up. He was fixing dinner at home too. Menial tasks, at home, were honorable.

He took three trips to Europe in the last ten years. All without his wife. During the last one he went to Rome, called his wife, and she said she was moving out again. He got into a panic, went to Sicily, painted five paintings and caught a plane home. He was gone five days.

Amid the ruins

79. STREET IN SPAIN
Oil on canva
24" x 30"

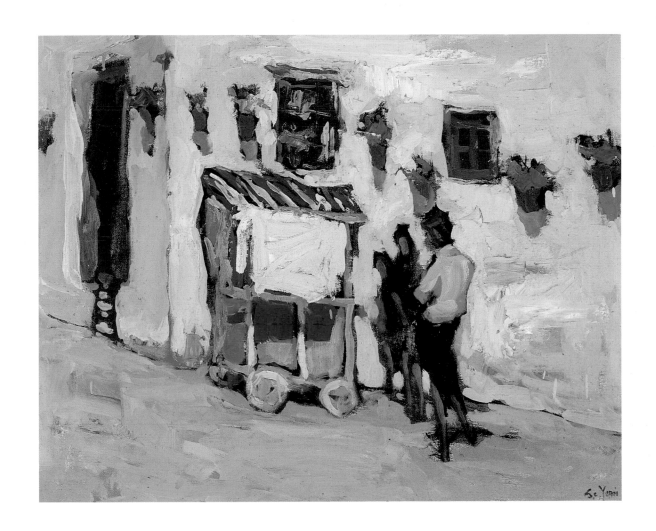

49. TIDE POOLS
   Oil on masonite
   11" x 24"
   This painting has a piece
   of gravel, from Yuan's
   driveway, lodged in the
   middle of the canvas.

37. BOATS,
   Oil on masonite
   15" x 18"

In China the husband has all the rights. Yuan never got used to it here. Everything was left lying around in the house for when he needed it. Mrs. Yuan was the opposite. She was the one who wanted the big house. He helped the contractor build the house. He painted and did all the jobs that the professionals did not have time to do. Signs of his painting would be everywhere. You would see painting materials lying in the yard. Some of his paintings were in the back yard, and his dog chewed them up. He would have as soon lived in an old house. But the new house was where Mrs. Yuan would come to him. So his environment was functional only, and Mrs. Yuan wanted something more. At the end, Yuan confided in my friend, Brenda, that his wife had just now learned that he loved her, after twenty–three years of marriage.

When Yuan and others went to a cafe to talk, Yuan bought something for everyone. Even if the person did not want it. He said that one must pay for the space. He was very thoughtful of the owner.

I would find myself talking like him in short, choppy sentences. If you said the wrong thing to Yuan you might find out later, that he would never speak to you again. Many people in Carmel lost his friendship and he never looked their way again.

—————————

Yuan was having a very hard time with what was in his mind, and what was fact. He said Mrs. Yuan was getting all the property and leaving him in the street.

Two months ago, Yuan said that he had enough money to pay his bills for the next two years. He would paint for these two years, and at the end of this time, he would return to China, never to paint again, but work in the fields of China. He said that one should be able to labor at a regular job for eight hours, come home and paint another eight hours. This means four paintings in this time span.

Mrs. Yuan said the lawyers were looking for Yuan's will. Y. S. Lim said, "There is no will." Lim said today, that Yuan said when he

75. CANNERY ROW
    Oil on board
    12" x 16"

HELEN DOOLEY

Artist, teacher, and gallery owner, Helen Dooley (1907–1993), wrote this letter to the Carmel Pine Cone just after Yuan's death. Carmel Pine Cone, September 19, 1974.

Dear Editor:

One of the greatest tributes any artist can receive is to have other artists buy his works.

This has happened to our great beloved friend, S. C. Yuan; unfortunately, it happened too late for him to see. In his greatest hour of desperation, he apparently, unknowingly created some of his greatest works, now hanging in his last one–man show in the Carmel Art Association.

Last Sunday after his tragic passing, every painting in the show was bought by friends, mostly artist friends, of Yuan. Each painting was a masterpiece. Yet he, it is said, was unhappy with his show.

The gnawing question is, why did we have to wait until he was gone to buy them?

The path of every truly great artist is a lonely one. Often unappreciated, the artist has to cut his own road, doing things differently from what has gone before, often enduring the agony of seeing his works passed by while lesser artists seem "successful."

Yuan was successful in the true sense of the word. He worked with a sincere passion, putting his life's blood and total energy into the work, developing a masterful and monumental form.

Yuan won awards here and elsewhere, many of which, went un-noticed here. He also sold well. Yet few can realize the depths of despair he must have gone through when his own standards were so high he felt he could never attain them.

Perhaps there are some aspects on Yuan. Difficult to understand, he needed people, he craved communication, but the finely–tuned sensitivity of the artist created a great gulf between him and his friends.

Yuan's friends loved him deeply, nevertheless, and his artist friends know they have lost one of the greatest artists who ever tread the paths of Monterey and Carmel to immortalize them in his paintings. ☞

111. UNTITLED
Oil on canvas
20" x 30"

Yuan's Years in China

1911	Manchu government overthrown. China declared a republic.
1912	Sun Yat–sen briefly serves as first president. Nationalist Party (Kuomintang) formed.
1916	Warlord period begins.
1921	Chinese Communist Party (CCP) founded.
1925	Death of Sun Yat–sen. Chiang Kai–shek becomes leader of the Nationalist Party.
1926–27	Joint Communist and Nationalist expedition against warlords is successful, but ends in division of the two parties.
1931	Japanese attack Chinese forces at Mukden.
1934–35	Long March of the Communists into the northwest.
1938	Nationalist capital is moved from Nanking to Chungking.
1942	The U. S. having entered World War II, sends aid to Nationalist government in Chungking through Burma.
1945	Japan surrenders.
1946–49	Civil war between the Nationalists and the Communists.
1949	Nationalist government surrenders. Chiang Kai–shek flees to Taiwan. Mao Tse–Tung (Mao Zedong) proclaims the establishment of the People's Republic of China.

Note:

While working on this project, we ran into the problem of spelling Chinese names in English. We would look for a province or a city in an atlas and not be able to find it. The spelling in English of Chinese names, cities and provinces has undergone changes in recent years, as the current Chinese government has attempted to set a standard spelling for Western languages. Before that, there were many ways to write out a name. Yuan's teacher, Xu Beihong is an example. After frustrating attempts to find out more about him, we found him listed in dictionaries and books under, not only Xu Beihong, but Peon Ju, Jupeon, Hsu Pei–hung and Siu Pei–hong. There probably are even more. Therefore, we have used on this map the *old spelling* that would have been in use, when Yuan was in China, and underneath it the current spelling. If we have offended anyone with an erroneous Chinese spelling in this catalogue, we apologize.

Sources

Benezit, E. *Dictionnaire des Peintres, Sculpteurs, Dessinateurs et Graveurs.* Vol. 10 Librairie Grund, Paris, 1976

Cohen, Joan Lebold. *The New Chinese Painting, 1949–1986.* Harry N. Abrams, New York, 1987

——————————————, and Jerome Alan Cohen. *China Today and Her Ancient Treasures.* 3rd. ed. rev., Harry N. Abrams, New York, 1986

Hookham, Hilda. *A Short History of China.* New American Library, New York, 1972

Sullivan, Michael. *The Arts of China.* University of California Press, Berkeley and Los Angeles, 1973

——————————————, *Chinese Art in the Twentieth Century*, University of California Press, Berkeley and Los Angeles, 1959

"Army Language School Instructor in Mandarin Chinese Exhibits Paintings", Irene Alexander. *Monterey Peninsula Herald*, May 29, 1953

"East and West Mingle in S. C. Yuan Exhibit", Irene Alexander. *Monterey Peninsula Herald*, January 22, 1958

"Abstractism Not Art Says Chinese Painter, It Doesn't Communicate." *Carmel Pine Cone– Cymbal*, August 20, 1959

"Couple at Work: Yuans Mix Art, Science, Cuisine." *Monterey Peninsula Herald*, June 24, 1961

"Sensitive Paintings by S. C. Yuan on Display," Irene Alexander. *Monterey Peninsula Herald*, February 14, 1962

"Yuan Shown in N.Y.C." *Carmel Pine Cone*, May 16, 1968

"Yuan's Works Meld Western, Oriental." Irene Alexander. *Monterey Peninsula Herald*, July 26, 1968

"Leo Braico, S. C. Yuan Featured at Carmel Art Association." *The Pine Cone*, May 11, 1972

"Artist S. C. Yuan Found Dead of Gunshot Wound." *Monterey Peninsula Herald*, September 7, 1974

"Private Rites Set for S. C. Yuan." *Monterey Peninsula Herald*, September 8, 1974

"Show Features Late Artist." *Carmel Pine Cone*, September 12, 1974

"Letters." *Carmel Pine Cone*, September 19, 1974

"Memorial Exhibition Honors Late Carmel Artist S. C. Yuan." *Monterey Peninsula Herald*, August 17, 1975

"S. C. Yuan, His Work is His Presence." *Carmel Pine Cone*, December 30, 1976

"Yuan Memorial Exhibit Opens at Winters Gallery." *Carmel Pine Cone/Carmel Valley Outlook*, May 20, 1982

Jen–Chi Anderson
John Yuan

Archives of the Carmel Art Association
Archives of the Monterey Peninsula Museum of Art
Archives of the Monterey Public Library
Archives of Philip and Madalyn Johnson
Archives of Dolores Johnson
Archives of Who's Who in Art, Monterey

65. POINT LOBOS FROM HIGHLANDS INN
Oil on canvas
21" x 27"
*Yuan painted this painting from the driveway of
the Highlands Inn, when he worked there as a
cook. Yuan gave this painting to Robert James
Ramsey, Sr., who at that time owned the Inn.*

Exhibition List

1. **CONWAY SUMMIT #2**
   Oil on canvas, 10" x 36"
   Collection of Barry K. Berghorn

2. **UNTITLED**
   Oil on paper, 24" x 24"
   Collection of Mr. and Mrs. William R. Avery

3. **BEACH SCENE**
   Oil on board, 14 1/2" x 19 1/4"
   Collection of Mr. and Mrs. William R. Avery

4. **PINE TREES**
   Oil on board, 24" x 12"
   Collection of Pat Antonio

5. **ST. MICHAEL'S, PARIS**
   Oil on canvas, 30" x 30"
   Private Collection

6. **STREET RONDA, OLD RING**
   Oil on canvas, 24" x 30"
   Private Collection

7. **RED BOUGAINVILLEA**
   Oil on canvas, 40" x 52"
   Collection of Mr. and Mrs. Y. S. Lim

8. **SNOW SIERRA**
   Oil on canvas, 36" x 60"
   Collection of Mr. and Mrs. Y. S. Lim

9. **MARIGOLDS**
   Oil pastel, 20" x 16"
   Collection of Mr. and Mrs. Y. S. Lim

10. **STILL LIFE WITH BOWL OF FRUIT**
    Oil on canvas, 20" x 24"
    Collection of Mr. and Mrs. Y. S. Lim

11. **POTTED FLOWER WITH LONG BLACK TRAY**
    Oil on board, 16" x 20"
    Collection of Mr. and Mrs. Y. S. Lim

12. **TWIN PINES**
    Oil on canvas, 60" x 40"
    Collection of Mr. and Mrs. Y. S. Lim

13. **IRENE KNITTING**
    Oil on canvas, 30" x 40"
    Collection of Mr. and Mrs. Y. S. Lim

14. **GIRL AT THE SUNNY SHORE**
    Oil on canvas, 32" x 48"
    Collection of Mr. and Mrs. Y. S. Lim

15. **THREE DEER ON THE SNOW**
    Watercolor on paper, 14" x 19"
    Collection of Mr. and Mrs. Y. S. Lim

16. **SYMPHONY OF SUNSHINE**
    Oil on burlap, mounted on board, 30" x 40"
    Collection of Mr. and Mrs. Y. S. Lim

17. **MEDITERRANEAN MARKET**
Oil on board, 12" x 16"
Collection of Mr. and Mrs. Y. S. Lim

18. **VETERAN CYPRESS**
Oil on canvas, 60" x 80"
Collection of Mr. and Mrs. Y. S. Lim

19. **CHEVRON STATION, CARMEL**
Oil on board, 12" x 16"
Collection of Mr. and Mrs. Y. S. Lim

20. **HORSE AND FIGURE # 2**
Ink and chalk on paper, 8" x 8"
Collection of Mr. and Mrs. Y. S. Lim

21. **FIGURE ON CHAIR**
Charcoal on paper, 15" x 21"
Collection of Mr. and Mrs. Y. S. Lim

22. **SEATED FIGURE # 3**
Ink on paper, 10" x 8 1/2"
Collection of Mr. and Mrs. Y. S. Lim

23. **FIGURE BENDING OVER**
Ink and chalk on paper, 10" x 8 1/2"
Collection of Mr. and Mrs. Y. S. Lim

24. **MONTEREY BAY**
Oil on canvas, 54" x 78"
Private Collection

25. **WINTER, PARIS**
Oil on board, 16" x 20"
Collection of John K. M. Olsen

26. **CYPRESS**
Oil on board, 12" x 16"
Collection of John K. M. Olsen

27. **FISHERMEN**
Oil on canvas, 32" x 48"
Collection of John K. M. Olsen

28. **RECLINING NUDE**
Oil on canvas over board, 24" x 42"
Collection of John K. M. Olsen

29. **MARBELLA, SPAIN**
Oil on canvas, 26" x 31"
Collection of John K. M. Olsen

30. **MERRY PEACH**
Oil on canvas, 18" x 24"
Collection of John K. M. Olsen

31. **CARMEL**
Oil on canvas, 30" x 36"
Collection of Gil and Stephanie Day

32. **WEST COAST**
Oil on masonite, 30" x 40"
Collection of Mr. and Mrs. Thomas Tonkin

33. **LOOKOUT GATE**
Oil on board, 22 1/2" x 32"
Private collection

34. **UNTITLED**
Oil on masonite, 30" x 40"
Collection of Dr. and Mrs. Philip Thorngate

35. **UNTITLED**
Oil pastel and ink on paper, 24" x 18"
Collection of Harry Parashis

36. **TREES IN WINTER**
Oil on masonite, 23 1/2" x 23"
Collection of Mr. and Mrs. Marshall Hydorn

37. **BOATS**
Oil on masonite, 15" x 18"
Collection of Richard and Bonnie Forrester

38. **SAN MIGUEL DE ALLENDE**
Oil on canvas, 24" x 30"
Collection of Mr. and Mrs. Bruce J. Christensen

39. **RECLINING LADY IN HAT**
Ink on paper, 8 1/2" x 14"
Collection of Mr. and Mrs. Bruce J. Christensen

40. **HORSES**
Ink on paper, 4 1/2" x 10"
Collection of Mr. and Mrs. Bruce J. Christensen

41. **FIVE HORSES**
Oil on canvas, 25" x 31"
Collection of Mr. and Mrs. Thomas Ewen

42. **BIRD ON A BRANCH**
Oil on canvas, 44" x 43 3/4"
Collection of Mr. and Mrs. Thomas Ewen

43. **WATSONVILLE BARN**
Oil on canvas, 44" x 43 3/4"
Collection of Mr. and Mrs. Thomas Ewen

44. **CARMEL STREET SCENE, KIP'S MARKET**
Oil on masonite, 11 1/2" x 15 1/2"
Collection of Robert and Esther Anderson

45. **BLACKSMITH SHOEING HORSE**
Oil on masonite, 16" x 13"
Collection of Walter Georis

46. **PORTRAIT OF WALTER GEORIS**
Conte crayon on paper, 16" x 13"
Collection of Walter Georis

47. **WOMAN IN CHAIR**
Oil on board, 16" x 20"
Collection of Mr. and Mrs. Dean Jacobs

48. **PIER IN MONTEREY**
Oil on board, 14" x 18"
Collection of Mr. and Mrs. Dean Jacobs

49. **TIDE POOLS**
Oil on masonite, 11" x 24"
Collection of Steve Zembsch and
Deborah Hillyard

50. **COASTAL CYPRESS**
Oil on masonite, 18" x 14"
Collection of Steve Zembsch and
Deborah Hillyard

51. **REVOLUTION**
Collage on canvas, 29 1/2" x 96"
Collection of Mrs. Jen–Chi Anderson

52. **BOUGAINVILLEA**
Oil on canvas, 23 1/2" x 71 3/4"
Collection of Mrs. Jen–Chi Anderson

53. **SPANISH STREET**
Oil on board, 7 1/2" x 9 1/2"
Collection of Mrs. Jen–Chi Anderson

54. **MEETING**
Oil on board, 7 1/2" x 9 1/2"
Collection of Mrs. Jen–Chi Anderson

55. **ABSTRACT**
Oil on canvas, 32 1/2" x 32 1/2"
Collection of Ms. Rae Yuan

56. **SEASCAPE**
Oil on canvas, 6 1/2" x 18 1/2"
Collection of Ms. Rae Yuan

57. **SNOW, SIERRA**
Mixed media on canvas, 60" x 30"
Collection of Ms. Rae Yuan

58. **SICILY**
Oil pastel on paper, 13 1/2" x 18 1/2"
Collection of Mrs. Jen–Chi Anderson

59. **HORSES**
Oil on canvas, 7 1/2" x 31 3/4"
Private collection

60. **WHARF, MONTEREY**
Oil on canvas, 30" x 59"
Private collection

61. **SUNDAY FISHERMAN**
Oil on canvas, 24 1/2" x 54 1/4"
Private collection

62. **PARIS WINTER, # 3**
Oil on canvas, 16" x 20"
Collection of Mr. and Mrs. Richard J. Sneed

63. **WATERLILIES**
Oil on canvas, 17" x 48"
Collection of Dr. Robert A. Doyle

64. **SWEET PEAS**
Oil on board, 20" x 16"
Collection of Mrs. Elizabeth Hughes

65. **POINT LOBOS FROM HIGHLANDS INN**
Oil on canvas, 21" x 27"
Collection of Mrs. Robert James Ramsey, Sr.

66. **BLUE VASE**
Oil on canvas, 24" x 20"
Collection of Elva M. Bumb

67. **THE GINZA, RAINY DAY IN TOKYO**
Oil on burlap, 36" x 48"
Collection of Mrs. Janice O'Brien

68. **CARMEL HIGHLANDS**
Oil on board, 26 1/2" x 64"
Collection of Mr. and Mrs. W. F. Schmied

69. **VILLAGE STREET SCENE**
Oil on canvas, 8" x 11"
Collection of Mr. and Mrs. W. F. Schmied

70. **VIEW OF MONTEREY BAY**
Oil on board, 35 1/2" x 47 1/2"
Collection of Trotter Galleries, Carmel

71. **BREEZE**
Oil on canvas, 39" x 49"
Collection of Tom and Nancy Christie

72. **UNTITLED**
Watercolor on paper, 20 1/2" x 27 1/2"
Collection of Dr. and Mrs. William McAfee

73. **UNTITLED**
Collage on board, 31" x 26"
Collection of Mr. and Mrs. Howard Bucquet

74. **FOGGY MORNING**
Oil on canvas on masonite, 30" x 40"
Collection of Steve Zembsch and
Deborah Hillyard
Courtesy of Who's Who in Art

75. **CANNERY ROW**
Oil on board, 12" x 16"
Collection of Gerald Byrne

76. **CAFÉ RAOUL**
Oil on board, 18" x 24"
Collection of Gerald Byrne

77. **PARIS**
Oil on board, 20" x 30"
Collection of Gerald Byrne

78. **WINTER, SPAIN**
Oil on board, 26" x 31"
Collection of Gerald Byrne

79. **STREET IN SPAIN**
Oil on canvas, 24" x 30"
Collection of Gerald Byrne

80. **SEASCAPE**
Oil on board, 12" x 24"
Collection of Gerald Byrne

81. **TILLIE GORTS**
Pen and chalk on paper, 9" x 11 1/2"
Collection of Gerald Byrne

82. **UNTITLED**
Watercolor on paper, 29 1/4" x 15"
Collection of Eleanor Hatlo Lusignan

83. **POUNDING SURF**
Oil on canvas on board, 34" x 44"
Collection of La Porte's Fine Art

84. **RAIN IN SPAIN**
Oil on canvas, 36" x 48"
Collection of Mr. Hitoshi Kono

85. **RAIN**
Watercolor on paper, 15" x 14"
Collection of Mr. Hitoshi Kono

86. **CASTROVILLE #2**
Oil on canvas, 24" x 36"
Private Collection

87. **PORTRAIT OF RAE**
Oil on canvas, 36" x 35 1/2"
Private Collection

88. **EVENING CLOUDS**
Oil on canvas, 12" x 16"
Private Collection

89. **GLADIOLAS**
Oil on canvas, 40" x 40"
Private Collection

90. **STILL LIFE WITH RED ROSES**
Oil on canvas, 20" x 16"
Private Collection

91. **HUNTER'S POINT**
Oil on board, 10" x 23"
Private Collection

92. **HEAD # 2**
Pastel on paper, 15" x 12"
Private Collection

93. **SEASCAPE**
Oil on masonite, 8 1/2" x 23 3/8"
Private Collection

94. **HEAD # 1**
Pastel on paper, 15" x 12"
Private Collection

95. **THREE BOATS**
Oil on board, 18" x 24"
Private Collection

96. **UNTITLED**
Oil on board, 8" x 10"
Private Collection

97. **GRAPEFRUIT AND GRAPES**
Oil on board, 8" x 10"
Private Collection

98. **THREE ORANGES AND PEARS**
Oil on board, 16" x 20"
Private Collection

99. **CASTROVILLE**
Oil on board, 9" x 12"
Private Collection

100. **ARTICHOKE STAND**
Oil on board, 9" x 12"
Private Collection

101. **MONTEREY WHARF**
Oil on masonite, 12" x 16"
Collection of Mrs. Robert J. Kaller

102. **STILL LIFE WITH RED ROSE**
Oil on masonite, 8" x 10"
Collection of Mr. and Mrs. David Davis
Courtesy of Trotter Galleries, Carmel

103. **PORTRAIT**
Oil on board, 12" x 12"
Collection of Mrs. Margaret Tennison

104. **SUNNY BAY**
Oil on canvas, 24" x 36"
Collection of Edward and Alison Marouk

105. **PINE TREES**
Oil on canvas, 36" x 60 1/2"
Collection of Sheila Sheppard and
Gaston Georis

106. **SAN FRANCISCO**
Oil pastel on paper, 6" x 10"
Collection of Sheila Sheppard and
Gaston Georis

107. **UNTITLED**
Ink on paper, 10 1/2" x 18 1/2"
Collection of John Ishizuka

108. **THE SEA**
Oil on canvas, 22" x 31 1/4"
Collection of The Monterey Peninsula
Museum of Art
Gift of Mr. and Mrs. William G. Hyland

109. **SUNBATHERS**
Oil on canvas, 18" x 24"
Collection of Mr. Eugene Rogalsky

110. **ON A BLUE PLATE**
Oil on panel, 12" x 16"
Collection of Mr. Eugene Rogalsky

111. **UNTITLED**
Oil on canvas, 20" x 30"
Collection of Mr. and Mrs. Barry Brown

Acknowledgments

The Carmel Art Association's Board of Directors, general membership and the Exhibition Committee wish to sincerely thank the individuals and organizations who have generously loaned works for this special exhibition; all of the Association's members and friends, who have given their time to work on the fundraiser, monitor the exhibition room, and assist with the mailings.

A special thanks to Jen–Chi Anderson, Rae Yuan and John Yuan. Their help has been invaluable. We also wish to thank Dick Crispo, Walter Georis, Sam Harris, Dolores Johnson, Delores Kaller, Hitoshi Kono, Y. S. Lim, Keith Lindberg, Claudia Peterson, Rollin Pickford, Sheila Sheppard, Gerald Wasserman, and Sjef Wildschut for their stories. Their memories and help have added greatly to this exhibition and catalogue.

In addition, we wish to thank Phil Thorngate, our 1994 CAA president, for all his help and last-minute fact gathering; Bill Stone, for doing a fine job producing the map for the catalogue; Will Bullas for coming to our aid, despite his busy schedule, with good spirits and encouragement; Frieda Golding for her very good advice; Jim Johnson for remembering us when he found the old *Carmel Pine Cone*s; Frank Herwatt for getting our computers ready just in time; and to the CAA staff, Janet Howell, Karen Lyon, Harry Shelby and Barbara Smith for all the extra time and energy they have had to put in, in order to make this all work.

And to our good and persistent friend, Walter Nelson–Rees, our sincerest thanks for all his hard work and uncompromising attention to detail. It has been comforting to know he was only a fax away.

This catalogue is made possible in part by generous donations from:

> Anonymous supporters
> Mr. Gerald Byrne
> Mr. and Mrs. Howard Bucquet
> Mr. Harrison Gonsalves
> Mrs. Taher Obaid
> The Barnet Segal Trust
> Terry and Paula Trotter, Trotter Galleries, Carmel

Black and white photographs courtesy of Steve Crouch Jr., Walter Georis, Sam Harris, Y. S. Lim, Claudia Peterson, Sjef Wildschut, and John Yuan.

Drawings in margins courtesy of Y.S. Lim.

Exhibition Committee

Brenda Morrison, Chairman
Gael Donovan, Director
Wilda Northrop
Margaret Roberts, Archivist
Dennis Wyszynski, Staff Photographer